A Privileged Life II

Wisdom from My Journey

Tom,
I am very grateful to you
for being a part of my life.
Hope as you read, something
we have shared will also be
gained wisdom.
Love & admiration
Delores
5/19

Praise for:
A Privileged Life II
Wisdom from My Journey

A Privileged Life II – Wisdom from My Journey defines a Spirit-led woman of God, possessing light, strength, purpose and wisdom, so, so much wisdom. I am proud to call Mrs. "B" "Mom," Friend, Mentor, Teacher and Counselor. I am grateful for over 45 years of her pulling me closer so she could then push me out, better than when I arrived.

Mary C. Tutt Garrett
Executive Assistant to Delores F. Brisbon
Philadelphia, PA

I really enjoyed the whole book! Perhaps the most true statement I can make about my grandmother, Delores Brisbon, is that I've always known her to be exactly who she is. In *A Privileged Life II - Wisdom from My Journey,* she examines the source of that authenticity and how her intense faith has directed each phase of her life. Though introduced as a book intended to mentor others, A Privileged Life II reads at its heart as a love letter - to her late husband James; to the personal relationships that formed her; and, above all, to God, the Divine Spirit who has guided her through eight decades of living in faith.

Abby Brisbon
University of PA, C'09
Bachelor of Arts in History
Philadelphia, PA

Delores Brisbon, I am thankful for your wisdom and ability to give of yourself. Each one of us who know you has benefited on a personal, professional and spiritual level. The wisdom drawn from your remarkable life now included in this one book offers a guide for more and more to live an authentic and more spiritually satisfying life. You have shared your inner and outer self fully and completely. The reflections, lessons, stories and prayers are meditations that can be used as a daily guide – it's a pocket mentor to carry with you always. It is a treasure to be shared with those we know and love.

Lynette M. Brown-Sow
Consultant
LM Brown Management Group, LLC
Philadelphia, PA

Delores' book is a primer for life, reflecting the experience and wisdom that she has shared as my friend, mentor, and Christian mother. Delores has taught me the foundation of her authentic excellence: God, faith, and marriage and family, in that order. I aspire to live the integrated, prayerful life that Delores has taught.

Roselyn Hseuh, Ph.D.
Associate Professor, Department of Political Science
Co-Advisor, Certificate in Political Economy
College of Liberal Arts, Temple University
Philadelphia, PA

Authentic. Direct. Confident. God-centered. Spirit-guided. Wise. Dr. Delores Brisbon's true essence and character come alive in this her second book, *A Privileged Life II – Wisdom From My Journey*. Over the past decade, I have been professionally and personally blessed by her consultation with the In Trust Center for Theological Schools. Dr. Brisbon is a master at sharing her wisdom with colleagues, friends, family, and others who are seeking to grow and develop in their own leadership and life. For those who know and love her and for those seeking wisdom from a successful, proven executive leader and strategist, this book offers a map, a structural guide, to leading from one's core and using one's God-given gifts in the service of others.

Dr. Brisbon provides an authentic example of living and leading guided by Christian values and God's word. As a witness to her practice, I can attest to the truth in these pages while also learning and appreciating new aspects of her journey as a pioneer. Dr. Brisbon is a blessing to those she serves – her church, her organizations, her mentees, her family and friends, and her community. She has an endless capacity to give and her generosity of wisdom is evident whether you experience her in person or only in the pages of this book. Use it as a reference when seeking wisdom in your personal or professional life. I am honored and blessed to do so.

Amy L. Kardash
President
In Trust Center for Theological Schools
Wilmington, DE

A Privileged Life II – Wisdom from My Journey has fed my soul. Delores reminds me in this book of the joy of daily conversations with God – the joy, patience and caring. God listens.

Letty Roth Piper, EdD, MSN, RN
Assistant Professor
Director, Strategies for Success Program
LaSalle University
Philadelphia, PA

As this memoir reveals, Dr. Brisbon is a powerful, charismatic woman of color who uses her God-given gifts to live out God's plan for all of us: 'Love God, love your neighbor, and love yourself.' Her life long relationship with God has enabled her to realize her neighbor includes even strangers and enemies. As a result, she has given God permission to empower her to meet her challenges in life and those people who have challenged her with confidence, grace, and forgiveness, 'free of anger and bitterness'. Her mantra is 'Be yourself. Respect yourself and others.' She is "the real deal."

Mike Pulsifer
Retired Presbyterian Minister and Neighbor
Philadelphia, PA

The narrative is enriched and continues to be inspiring and insightful. I am compelled to work with more diligence at my craft and the application of my gifts because of Delores' high standards of excellence and her passionate investment of caring wisdom!

Grace and peace,

Vergel L. Lattimore, Ph.D. President
Professor of Pastoral Psychology and Counseling
Hood Theological Seminary
Salisbury, NC

With a gentle quietness and firm confidence, Delores shares with any and all who will hear from the fullness of a life well and richly lived. Wisdom accompanies her every word and chapter and I gained in mind, body and spirit from every word.

I moved from chapter to chapter, eager to find what I would glean next in these pages, precious gems born of a phenomenal life, experiences of exquisite joy and intense pain, saturated with the presence of God. Delores' generosity of spirit and keenness of mind, as she has moved from age to age, with a familial and mentoring loving kindness, astounds and fills my heart. In written word as in life, Delores never ceases to amaze. In reading more of her life's lessons for we too who hunger and thirst, my soul cries out hallelujah! I give God thanks for Delores!

The Rev. Alton B. Pollard, III, Ph.D.
President, Louisville Presbyterian Theological Seminary
Louisville, Kentucky

A Privileged Life II - Wisdom from My Journey is a rare example of personal transparency and an individual's faith journey. Its depth and candor goes far beyond the surface conversation that is all too common today. However, anyone who has had the privilege of knowing the author will not be surprised by the honesty and forthrightness of the story. This is a story of faith told by a woman of profound faith.

This small book is packed with so many profound insights across so many areas of life that it cannot be easily defined, categorized or summarized. However, while undergirded by a personal faith narrative, two wisdom themes seem to be ever present throughout this work. The first is the absolute necessity of knowing and valuing oneself. This knowing and valuing is grounded in an awareness of who one is in God. That awareness allowed Delores to accept herself as someone who was "different" at an early age and it kept her focused in high school and during her years as a nursing student at Tuskegee Institute. Ironically, her self-awareness was the basis for both her ability to write, "when we agree to the covenant of marriage, we are no longer our own" and it gave her the independence and strength to overcome the destructive force of racism she encountered through her life. Her self-awareness and self-valuing was especially needed in the face of the pervasive racism she encountered during her years of leadership at the University of Pennsylvania Hospital (HUP). Loving God and loving ones' authentic self are intermingled. That is wisdom from Delores.

The second wisdom theme that seemed to be present throughout this narrative is that life is made meaningful and worthwhile through living for others. Delores Brisbon has been the embodiment of that theme. Her faith relationship with God as demonstrated in her prayer life and study of scripture has led her to the conviction that loving and compassionate service to others is a reflection and result of her relationship with God. This is not a novel insight but this book makes the connection clear.

There is far more I could say, but as my wife and I approach our 50th wedding anniversary, I celebrate Delores' wisdom on marriage. Her words resonate with my continued experience of learning in marriage. I have a much greater appreciation for her wisdom now that I could have imagined possible when I said "I do" in August of 1969.

Thank you, Delores, for sharing *Wisdom from Your Journey.* Your wisdom helps make our journeys easier.

Edward L. Wheeler, M.Div., Ph.D.
President
Interdenominational Theological Center
Atlanta, GA

A Privileged Life II

Wisdom from My Journey

DELORES F. BRISBON

Foreword by

Eve J. Higginbotham-Williams,

SM, MD. Vice Dean for Penn Medicine Office of Inclusion and Diversity, Perelman School of Medicine University of Pennsylvania

For other copyright permissions, see pp. 163

ISBN: 978-0-9998819-7-2

For information about permissions or bulk purchases,
please contact
Delores Brisbon: deloresbrisbon2201@comcast.net

Zion Publishing Services
1500 Crown Colony Ct. #540
Des Moines, IA 50315
www.zionpublishing.org
Printed in the United States of America

Dedication

A Privileged Life II – Wisdom from My Journey is dedicated to my children both those genetic and those I have been privileged to be given – to those who call me mentor, friend, teacher, adviser, colleague, and to anyone who desires a life with God…

Prize wisdom highly
and exalt her,
and she will exalt you
and promote you;
she will bring you
to honor when you
embrace her.

Proverbs 4:8
(*The Amplified Bible*)

Table of Contents

Foreword

Oprah Winfrey once stated, "Surround yourself with only people who are going to lift you higher."[1] For the last 10 years, I have been fortunate enough to have Delores Brisbon as one of my circle of friends who has lifted me higher. Her latest book, *A Privileged Life II – Wisdom From My Journey,* provides an open door for others to experience the inspired existence of my "big sister," Delores. Through a series of chapters, she ushers us through her life experiences, simultaneously sharing pearls of wisdom along the way.

There are a few highlights that I would like to share with you before you find a comfortable chair, a cup of tea, and a few quiet moments to absorb this book. Your journey quickly begins in the first few pages.

I love the Introduction as I journeyed along with her on my own journey through life, reflecting on my own years of formation, reaffirming there exists a kinship with the author, separated in years but not notable experiences.

---

1 Kelly-Gangi, C. A Woman's Book of Inspiration, Quotes of Wisdom and Strength. Falls River Press, 2017

I particularly enjoyed the way she used biblical verses and quotations expressing wisdom and a sense of acknowledgment that life is a journey. The inclusion of the inspired words from others creates a clarifying emphasis of key messages.

There is deep wisdom in the chapter, entitled "The Wisdom of Being Yourself," as one considers the reflection of the "hole in one's soul" and the opportunity to allow God's love to fill that hole. To know oneself, to be authentic and the joy of knowing that you are a gift and have gifts to share.

I loved the chapter entitled Leadership. Weaved within the threads of Delores' story, is the importance of sponsorship, mentorship, humility, and self-confidence. Servant leadership, although not explicitly expressed within the words, was present throughout her narrative.

She carries a theme of resiliency into the chapter on racism, a topic that is as relevant now as it was early in Delores' career. One of the most memorable sentences, among many others was the following: "Owning an institutional position is a trap for pain. Someone once told me "institutions have no loyalty." True, but we are to value ourselves, the work we do, and not expect acclaim. The work must speak for itself." I could not agree more.

Wisdom pours from the chapter on aging, as Delores presents a series of observations about the process. For those that may be much younger and may not have had the chance as yet to witness first-hand others' experiences in the later chapters of life, this is indeed an important lesson to learn, as we hope we are all fortunate to experience this stage, comes without fanfare but wondrous grace and glory.

The chapter entitled, "The Wisdom From Prayer" as well as the chapter preceding it, go hand in hand. I particularly like this chapter since Delores provides an understanding regarding the power of prayer. For those of us raised in other faiths, our prayer practice may have been taught to us differently, however, what Delores successfully accomplishes is to help us understand not only the power of prayer, but also how to tap into that power. Her personal journey, once again, provides an important understanding on how to navigate life's challenges in prayer and the mental journey one must take to access to quiet conversations with God. This chapter is my favorite.

A Privileged Life II – Wisdom from My Journey is a book that you will want to read multiple times. Consider it a "How To" manual for living an inspired life and you will benefit from precious observations and the wisdom imparted by my "big sister," Delores and gain invaluable insight that will last for years to come.

Eve J. Higginbotham-Williams, SM, MD
Vice Dean for Penn Medicine Office of
Inclusion and Diversity
Perelman School of Medicine
University of Pennsylvania
Philadelphia, PA

Introduction

Many people hesitate to talk about their faith or God to friends, colleagues or even family, especially in places where they are not likely to be believed. I am not one of those persons. I believe we talk about those matters closest to our hearts, that which we love. I love God and seek to emulate His teachings in my daily life. I have wanted to write about God's Power, to narrate a message that tells of His Power through the stories of my life. The stories in this book are the best I have to tell.

I carry out devotions (reading, meditating, reflecting) every morning - something I have done across seven decades. The Bible is my manual for living. I read, meditate and listen to the words with an intentional desire to learn. I use commentaries to clarify what I don't understand. I also read meditations and narratives written by others whose lives serve as mentors, among whom are Shirley Young, Oswald Chambers, Thomas Merton, Eugene Peterson, Mary Nilsen, Mark Nepo, the Upper Room Discipline, and a compilation of devotions written by a number of theologians and edited by Mary Tileston in 1897. I spend two hours in silence, reading, praying and listening.

One morning in late August 2017, during my time of devotion, words of the writer of the Gospel of Luke and Acts caught my attention and lingered in my mind for several days:

> *Many have undertaken to draw upon an account of things that have been fulfilled among us. With this in mind I decided to write an orderly account.*
>
> Luke 1:3-TNIV

I had been thinking about writing my second book since publishing my memoir in 2010. Sitting in my bedroom is a basket filled with legal pads which bears witness to my indecision. I have been encouraged by many who read A Privileged Life - Remembering my Journey, to write more, to “share wisdom" or to “tell us how you did that." My daughter-in-law, Janine, soon after reading my memoir asked me to “write your next book as a mentor." Chris Hall, who edited my memoir, suggested, “You should write your next book on lessons learned." My now deceased friend and co-worker across nine years of working together, the late Mark S. Levitan, encouraged me for many years to “tell your story.” While my memoir did tell my story, nothing motivated me to write again until I read this passage from Luke.

Shortly after deciding to write a second book, Emerson, my first-born grandchild, invited me to see the movie "Hidden Figures." Days later she asked, "What did you think about the movie?” Em is convinced that I am a hidden figure, and has asked that I write stories of my life, rather than reporting on their happenings. She is joined by a choir of voices that agree with her. I write now for all those who want to hear more from me, how I have moved through struggles, pain, and many difficulties and have emerged free of bitterness or anger.

In this book, I write the listed Lessons from my memoir: The Bible: A Power Beyond our Own; Prayer; Being Yourself; Marriage; Racism; Aging and Grief.

Luke, in the verse cited, is telling his audience that many had written first-hand accounts of their time with Jesus, accounts he had read, but he too had a story to tell. A physician, Luke knew the value of an accurate account of events. He was required to do so in the practice of medicine, to record treatment to his patients. People for two thousand years have read Luke's stories and been provided with knowledge about faith, guidance, wisdom, and spiritual growth, along with a history of the founding of the Christian Church.

Clearly, I am no Luke. I am, however, a nurse trained to accurately report events. In this book, A Privileged Life II - Wisdom from my Journey, I tell as accurately as I can stories of my life lived, guided and enriched by an inner spirit, stories of wisdom I have gained. I do not write as an authority on any subject, rather to share experiences that have over eight decades transformed my soul from an academic or intellectual understanding of life to a new life, which has given me a spirit of authenticity. There is a difference between knowledge and wisdom, although wisdom often includes knowledge, experiences and observations. However, the difference is the source. True wisdom has one source - God.

This book is not a research paper or platform for debate, although I hope it will be a source to those who seek to know themselves better by seeking true wisdom through their lived stories. I write to share, guide and advise seekers on their journey, hoping that God can use my words and my experiences to inform, guide or advise another. The experiences I speak in these pages have been a source of wisdom gained over a long life. Every story is personally owned. This book is for those who seek greater spiritual wisdom in their own lives.

I have read again and again my memoir, journals I have kept over the years, examined my musings, notes in the books I have read and highlighted and, to the extent I can, recalled events. I have lived a privileged life, not because of family background, education, money, achievements or acclamations, but rather by the Divine Order of God. What may appear to some as a unique set of circumstances or opportunities have defined my outer life. It is actually defined by inner spiritual direction. My source is Divine Spirit, whom I call upon to inform my daily decisions.

Everyone has a natural inner spirit which may or may not be connected to something beyond themselves. For me, the Power beyond my own comes from communion with the Spirit, which I learned about through Christianity.

The Holy Spirit cannot be defined; it is a mystery, difficult to understand and discounted by many who give credit to another source. I don't judge those persons, however, men and women who have received the Spirit live “in the world but not of the world" as recorded in the Gospel of John 17. We do not fit in a mold. While we may speak a prophetic word from God, we are not prophets. While we might preach God's word to those hungry to hear it, we are not preachers. We live from the inside out marching to a different beat. Like the biblical authors and apostles, we may or may not be intellectually gifted or formally educated. But God has touched us in a very special and unique way.

As a little girl, my spirit was connected to a Presence I could not see or hear, but could only experience. The messages sometimes frightened me, although they were never mean spirited or about anyone else, just about what I was to do. I did not fit among my peers. I grew up a studious girl sometimes labeled "old fashioned" or "old spirited" or just plain "odd." Fortunately, the wise women of the church nurtured this spirit and taught me it was of God. It took years for me to mature enough to believe these wise women. When I came to trust through biblical truth this inner self, I accepted and lived into a quiet guiding force, intricate in everything I do. It is not something to be explained, debated or called into being. I cannot take credit for it. I was and am obedient to the Guide.

For some people, Spirit can be debated, explained or theorized about. It cannot for me. During the years of early childhood development, college and my early professional career, I came to accept who I am. I have chosen to adapt my introverted spirit to accommodate what I needed to do, careful not to compromise its origin. I was a shy little girl, and as an adult, I am comfortable with aloneness, listening, quietness, and I am selective with whom I engage in human relations and with the kind of services I undertake. I am true to God, and to that child who was born with a gift for spiritual focus and resilience.

Being myself has been at the root of every natural achievement personally, professionally and socially. I was born in 1933 in Jacksonville, Florida when black people were less valued or not considered equal by white people. In some places in the southern United States, we were not considered human. Growing up in a family of eight children, four boys and four girls, my parents worked hard to feed, house, and keep us safe. However, more importantly, we were shaped to value ourselves. My parents did not deny racism and did not allow this evil to shape us. Our dominant shaping was in an environment of love modeled, spoken and spiritually enhanced.

I studied in segregated schools from books first used by white students. Every aspect of our lives was controlled by the segregated neighborhoods in which only black men, women and children made their homes. The Duval County school district had one high school for black youngsters, Stanton High School. Our classes were so large we were divided into sessions. In my class alone, we were divided into eight sessions. We may not have met a classmate until graduation if not taking subjects together. Our school graduated two classes a year each averaging 400 or more students. Our success was underpinned by our family, our communities, encouragement from and engagement in the church and teachers whose desire for us to become a success. More than anything, this background gave me the wisdom to be myself.

Formation matters; how we are shaped is who we are and it has made me who I am.

Fortunately for me, my parents, especially Daddy, believed I "could do whatever I wanted to." This one comment made to me by Daddy when I was 10 or 11 years old has been a foundation for the majority of my career decisions and, without question the security in which I engage male relationships. Wisdom gained while living in a marginalized external environment was balanced by a close-knit, internal space - sharing meals and clothing, laughing and praying, valuing the church and our neighbors. Growing up in this environment shaped a foundation for developing relationships, those that have been sustained and those that were not. Acceptance of individual choice, respect, love, and mutual purpose have been critical elements in developing relationships across my life, and a source of mental well-being.

When I graduated from the School of Nursing at Tuskegee University, I received an invitation from Mrs. Q.E. Carter for a position at the John Andrews Memorial Hospital in Tuskegee, Alabama, setting a pattern for the way I got my second job at the now-closed Flint-Goodridge Hospital in New Orleans, Louisiana. I was chosen for both these positions more because of the compassion I showed for patients and colleagues than my actual performance. Giving to and caring for others from a heart of love, a divine gift, is at the center of my service. In our current society, achievement, wealth, and ratings are more valued than caring. Wisdom informs me there is no match for love, kindness and compassion, no matter the course.

My longest professional job was at the Hospital of the University of Pennsylvania (HUP). I began work at HUP in 1959 when America was in a civil rights war. I experienced the pain of the 1968 murder of Rev. Dr. Martin Luther King, the 1963 night massacre of Medgar Evers, the 1963 murder of President John F. Kennedy, the 1964 murders of Andrew Goodman, Michael Schwerner and James Cheney, as well as less public deaths of many who died for our rights. The riots, fights, and fires were the evening news. In HUP, a place organized to care for others, there were only a few, all doctors of the medical staff, who offered support or even spoke to me. Nowhere across my life has there been more need for resilience, except during the time of losing my husband James.

Across thirty years, I worked, grew, learned, gained wisdom, navigated racism and succeeded in rising to an unimaginable organizational level. Many, including myself, continued questions of how a black nurse from the southern United States could, in 1979, become the first black person to lead the operations of an Ivy League medical school hospital in America, one of few women in this position in any type hospital except those governed by religious orders. Wisdom gained during over 26 years from 1959 to 1987 could be a book of stories alone; instead, the simple truth is it came about by my being myself, fueled by spiritual formation.

Despite racism, there was balance in the HUP environment. Men and women looked beyond my skin tone, and none more than the late Dr. Arnold S. Relman, who became an advocate. He and I developed a relationship which moved beyond professional designation of physician or nurse forming a friendship that lasted until he died. Samuel Thier, Dr. Ann Marie Chirico, Drs. Clayton Kyle, Robert Mayock and Sylvan Eisman supported my work and respected me professionally and personally. Wisdom gained from these relationships transcended race or gender and contributed to my well-being. This wisdom gained has given me balance in facing racism for 50 years, teaching me that all white or black people are not the same.

> *Proverbs, a Wisdom book of the Bible, "Train up a child in the way he (she) should go, and when he (she) is old he will not depart from it."*
>
> Proverbs 22:2 (NIV)

James and I reared a son, Edgar, and a daughter, Nancy. By any standard of measurement, they are two adults who honored the Fourth Commandment, "Honor your father and your mother" (Deuteronomy 5:16). Our children gave us grandchildren: Emerson, Abby and Welton. Rearing Edgar and Nancy afforded us opportunities to shape their lives and by extension their children. We were not interested in living our lives through our children nor did we place demands on who they were to be, rather we encouraged them to nurture and support the person they were created to be, not to achieve personal unfulfilled areas in our own lives. We did instill values of love, respect and caring which is evident in the professions they chose. Edgar is a counselor to seniors in transition and Nancy a family medicine physician.

I am not a stranger to horrific personal pain. My husband James died November 12, 2004. James and I lived in a marriage arranged by my maternal Aunt Remell. Our effortless, harmonious relationship expanded almost five decades, punctuated by deep, inner connections in almost every aspect of life. Our connectivity, fueled by love, sustained us through a horrific journey of 17 years with Alzheimer's Disease, which arrived in the 32nd year of our marriage. Our marriage gave me wisdom and understanding about things that matter. During our journey with Alzheimer's Disease, I gained wisdom of what "until death do us part" really meant, not just spoken in vows, but lived out in pain. The wisdom of pain suffered in the most intimate relationship of my being tested my will and spirit - yet in the years since James left, I have been gifted with resilience to live and to continue to contribute through Divine Spirit.

Now 86 years old, I have stories to tell, wisdom to share and just maybe, I am able to see more clearly the "hidden figure" Emerson wants me to discover. The stories are told in chapters, yet are intermingled, akin to life. Life is not lived in chapters but interwoven, making a long life such as my own a whole. This book is envisioned as a mentor for readers, giving meaning to others, as many have given to me.

~ One ~

The Bible
Our Only Source of Wisdom

Wisdom is a living stream, not an icon preserved in museums. Only when we find the spring of wisdom in our own life can it flow to future generations.

Thich Nhat in *The Book of Awakening* - Mark Nepo

Oswald Chambers said, "There is nothing mysterious or miraculous about the things we can explain." Chambers is right. God cannot be explained. I cannot see God; He is a mysterious and miraculous Spiritual Being experienced in my inner spirit. I have lived more than eight decades in this mysterious place knowing God is everywhere. I have gained wisdom that has become my living stream by reading, listening to and understanding the 66 Books God inspired men to write. Reading these sacred texts has, over and over again, revealed a Power beyond my own.

The Bible is the source to access God. Blessed with a long life of living well, I have been led by the Bible to believe, embrace, love and live in faith—the unseen Power of God. Learning from the Bible and from revelations in my spirit have given me wisdom to know that my views, thoughts, musings, intelligence, experiences and education are too limited to see the horizons of God. Living as prescribed by the words of the Bible has made me whole.

"Wisdom is understanding things as they are—me, God—and the way the world works." (J .Stephen Lang). Proverbs 11:8 (NLT) says that "Wisdom is more valuable than rubies. Nothing you desire can be compared with it." True wisdom has only one source—God—gained thorough intimacy with the Divine Being. Spending time with God taught me His character and I deliberately choose to follow where He may lead. Over the course of eight decades, God has become my go-to Source. Living in the highest priority intimate relationship with God has guided me through early formation, college, marriage, rearing children, being a grandmother, serving church and community, and to a surprisingly continuous professional career.

Spiritual Formation

Chris Hall, a notable scholar in Spiritual Formation, once told me, "We are formed by something; it is best when that is God." Formation sets pathways for our lives allowing us to grow, to change, and to live into that which God made us to be. We make choices which determine our destiny and even change our choice if the first choice does not fit. I have changed several times, but rarely moved away from the formation of my birth community, my family, or the church.

My Spiritual formation began in our home of four brothers and three sisters, watched over by a caring, praying Momma and hardworking, wise Dad, which underpins my adult, matured self. While I celebrate my early formation, I am aware that others may not have had the same experience. We who were born in oppressive, discriminating, segregated environments have had to make choices, some of which may not be common to others. My church community taught me that there was more in life than I could see, to not be defined by where or what I had or didn't have, rather to be defined by who I am, my authentic self.

I was born, and grew up, in rural Jacksonville, Florida, in the early 1930s. My world was confined to living in a small wood frame house of less than 1000 square feet on a dirt road called York Street, so named for a family who owned the largest area of that strip of land. Living in this space was the foundation to learning how to share with others and practice gratitude for materialistic goods. When I moved beyond our home, which was filled with praying and loving adults, discipline, expectations, abundant food, cleanliness and order, I emerged into an outer world of racial discrimination and the ugliness of segregation. In my home, we were only expected to be ourselves, using our gifts to serve others.

Our marginalized community of women and men, defined by the values of love, encouraged education and its importance. Even though they were not "trained" themselves, they wanted the best for us. Women like Mrs. Adeline Brown, my Godmother, Mrs. Frankie Thompson, Mrs. Rosa Smith, Mrs. Virginia Womack, and men like Rev. Saul Cooper, Mr. "Chuck" Thomas, and Mr. William Toombs taught and modeled "love God, neighbors and ourselves." These early mentors I call "precious gifts" modeled lives of biblical teaching by demonstrating how to live on the margins with dignity, and not be defined by the segregation and discrimination that structured, oppressed and disrespected our personhood.

> *"Love the Lord your God with all your passion and prayer and intelligence." This is the most important, the first on any list.*
>
> Matthew 22:37 (*The Message*)

A lack of respect from most whites, while designed to rob men and women of their humanity, did not - could not. I was surrounded by ordinary black working people defined by society as the low-middle class, earning meager wages, limitedly "trained," but a mecca of the best of humanity. While many in American society hold a view that black people live in dysfunctional families, unmarried mothers and folks who are less than, these views are wrong. York Street had eleven intact families, all with married parents living together who made God and family priority. These family structures were duplicated across our immediate community. Acceptance was the common behavior, not because we were black, but out of loving hearts.

Growing up in this small, contained area of rural Jacksonville, our lives were difficult—not even close to being privileged. We lived with biblical values, "God, neighbor, self." Putting others before ourselves was healthy and right. We were not codependent. Shaped to take care of my spirit meant giving and caring for others, as well as or better than myself. I learned how to serve others because of the love God gave me. Living into and practicing this concept has not meant dishonoring myself. It has meant being and giving based on an authentic relationship with God, informed through His inspired Word—the Bible. Biblical power has kept me focused, secure, bold, confident to serve with joy, peace, significant personal mental and physical health and professional success. The Spirit of God has been, and continues to be, the source of my strength, whether in times of joy, darkness or challenging spaces.

Living a Spirit-led life does not leave time or energy for comparing oneself with others, jealousy, competition, or seeking approval. My time is spent advancing others to greater horizons. I like to think of my life as "planting seeds in others" for them to become the best they can be.

...a man's spiritual health is exactly proportional to his love for God.

C. S. Lewis.

The Bible

I am shaped by the Bible more than any other resource, education, experience, or cultural exposure. Since I first learned to read the printed word, I have been a student of the Bible, the only book in our modest home.

Our family could not afford to buy magazines or newspapers. Before I read from my first book in school, I read Scripture. I was enchanted by the stories that God spoke audibly to humans such as Moses, telling him the" burning bush" was Holy Ground, or the stories of Abraham and Sarah, among others. I was a young adult before realizing that God was speaking to my heart through these Words. For many, many years, I searched for something I could not name, but in time, I realized it was beyond what I could see. Holy Scriptures led me to an understanding about my search. I was looking for God and I became a Bible-believing person.

I acknowledge not having always understood what I was reading which led me to read more. I had a thirst to know what the 66 books in the Bible were saying, the mysteries the content unfolded, and the power of love shown to humans despite disobedience. I did not need an education or to be an expert to read the Bible. I only needed an open, humble heart, to receive, believe and live the contents. When I have not understood, I ask the Author who is God. The Rev. Ulysses Bracy, with whom I studied Bible for three years, told me, "Read the Bible and change your life." My understanding of Scripture in early life was strengthened by sermons heard on Sunday as I worshiped in the small Jerusalem Baptist Church, or attended the African Episcopal or United Methodist churches in my community. As an adult, learning more through sermons has been a priority. In Monumental Baptist Church, Mother Bethel A.M.E. Church, and now as an aged Christian, at The First Presbyterian Church in Philadelphia. For me, Sunday morning is worship in church.

Many who read the Bible choose to see it only from a historic perspective. While I do not judge this perspective, if the Bible does not move history to contemporary times as a means to make life better for others, in my view, it does not meet the salient reasons God inspired the men to write. Great minds can debate, argue, teach, preach, or even lead from a personal interpretation of the Bible. These interpreters use Scripture to aggrandize themselves, often causing others who don't read Scripture to head down a slippery path of damage or even destruction. The Bible, in my view, is the only source for righteous living.

It is best interrupted by the Spirit of God through listening, asking, and receiving direction from the Holy Spirit.

I served on the University Board of Trustees with an embedded Seminary for more than a decade. We were often privileged to learn from the scholars who taught the students, being mindful of our responsibility to monitor the content of teaching and modeling. On one such occasion, we listened with awe as a scholar of the New Testament presented the Gospel to us. When questioning began, a colleague Trustee Bible teacher and medical doctor asked, "Where do you worship?" This scholar said, "I don't." It would be an understatement to say how disappointed we were. Because, you see, we believed the words of Timothy.

> *All Scripture is God-breathed [given by divine inspiration] and is profitable for instruction, for conviction [of sin], for correction [of error and restoration to obedience], for training in righteousness [learning to live in conformity to God's will, both publicly and privately—behaving honorably with personal integrity and moral courage];*
>
> 2 Timothy 3:16 (AMP)

The Bible is the transformational power to receive wisdom. I grew to appreciate that the time spent reading these inspired words of God inspired me to teach, guide and to gain wisdom to offer to others. I taught Sunday school during my teen and high school years and as an adult, and attended Bible classes. As I have taught and been taught, my wisdom increased. The Bible is more valuable than surfing the Internet, watching television, or engaging in dysfunctional conversations. The wisdom gained from reading the Bible is a life-changer when we choose to live the concepts.

Over the course of my life, I have seen and heard biblical passages used to justify many things, slavery among them, by persons who want to rewrite this Holy script. However, studying Scripture for myself with attentive prayerfulness has taught me that the Bible is not literature to be used to support particular ideas, life choices or life styles. People have used Scripture to twist the words to accommodate themselves, to begin cults and sects, even movements, by taking Scripture out of context. The best witnesses of the authority of the Bible are men and women whose lives testify to its truth. We either accept the wisdom from this Holy Book or reject its witness and content. We, who read the Bible in search of wisdom from God, know our lives have been changed. We are inspired to serve others because we have encountered God in the Scriptures and received the gift of love from Jesus, embracing Him as Savior of the world.

How to Read the Bible

Read the Bible with purpose, looking for a message. Seek to find your situation in the passage asking, "What does this teach me? Can I become a better person from knowing this? What am I to do with this message?" When encountering something not understood, reflect on the words, patiently reading them again. When clarity is slow in coming, pray, asking the Author, "What does this mean for me?"

Learning the Scriptures is not a quick pass-through. Study is required, sometimes commentaries are helpful, and conversations with other believers illuminating. The Bible is not a one-time-only read, it is a way of living intended for a lifetime, the way to wisdom.

I have come to the 'end of myself' many times reading Scripture, being comforted, no matter the discomfort, guided to new direction, challenged and chastised. In other words, I have allowed God the freedom to work in me. Reading complete stories has enhanced my understanding and changed distorted thoughts. I have gained wisdom from the Old Testament stories recorded in Genesis, and learned how to lament, pray and trust God by reading the Psalms. The Bible has been and continues to be my primary resource and inspiration to address personal needs, relationships with others, worry, the future, and even weak faith. The rich stories and parables of the Bible taught me how to live well because of the wisdom given.

The stories of Creation recorded in Genesis 1, and 2:13; Noah and the flood - Genesis 6, 7, and 8:6-22; the Ten Commandments in Deuteronomy 5; Abraham's offering of Isaac in Genesis 22:1-19 all offered wisdom of how God began this world, how He chose ordinary people, and how He uses us all—things that guide and focus me. The Gospels introduced me to Jesus. They taught me how He lived, suffered and died, providing the map for being a Christian, and what is required of me to live in the Power beyond my own.

Seeing God through People

The character of God is love. Reading the Bible reveals God's love expressed to me by others in my life.

Momma was the first person I heard call out to God for our daily needs, which were always met with abundance. People in my community offered encouragement and inspired me to go to college. As I neared graduation from high school, unknown to me, Mr. Ira Bryant, Mrs. Amy Currie and Miss Minnie Cade were searching for a college my parents could afford. My teachers reasoned that Tuskegee University would be a match; tuition was low and I could get a job to supplement the cost of my education. My teachers believed I would succeed because I would graduate ranking second in a class of close to 1000 students. They watched me travel five miles round trip by bus and on foot to school for four years. I had no idea how to apply for college. There was no college graduate in my family; I was the first in my family to earn a college degree. Welton, my oldest brother, completed college after a time of serving in the army and economically made my college education real.

Daddy's wisdom set the path for my career. He decided I would study nursing at Tuskegee. Children in my time did not challenge a parent's decisions. His wise decision was based on seeing more than I could see in my studious, no-nonsense, serious personality of no sophistication or worldliness. With almost no money for a college education for me, Daddy, with help from my brothers Welton and Willie, combined their funds enough for the entrance fee, first quarter tuition, and a train ticket to Opelika, Alabama. Daddy bought a cardboard suitcase, a new coat, a few clothes to supplement gifts from a woman I worked for and two pairs of shoes. I left home to attend Tuskegee University and became a nurse. Being a nurse has been the foundation to all of my professional achievements, many of which have not been specific to medical care but all of which have been about serving others.

> *Nothing is small or great in God's sight. Whatever He wills becomes great to us, however seemingly trifling; and if once the voice of conscience tells us that He requires anything of us, we have no right to measure its importance. On the other hand, whatever He would not have us do, however important we may think it is, is as nought to us.*
>
> (Jean Nicolas Grou)

The "hand of God" has been evident in all things across my years, none of which could have happened without God. Before I met God in the Bible during my study with Rev. Bracy, I attributed intellect, hard work and opportunity to myself. And while this was true, the order in which my life evolved was not precedented. I would not have been able to move through the ups and downs I faced as a black girl, born in a marginalized southern culture, poor, shy, introverted, with a spirit of aloneness, and significantly different from many around me. God guided my teachers, Daddy, my brothers, and the men and women in church and community to take me where He planned.

> *Trust in and rely confidently on the LORD with all your heart and do not rely on your own insight or understanding. In all your ways know and acknowledge and recognize Him, and He will make your paths straight and smooth [removing obstacles that block your way].*
>
> Proverbs 3:5-6 (AMP)

Seeing God

God is in the details of our lives. At Tuskegee, I excelled as a student in a spiritual environment that nurtured my quiet spirit and celebrated my mind. I did not fit in the social environment of parties, drinking, smoking, card playing, sneaking out of the dormitory, or events others seemed to enjoy. I worshiped on Wednesday evenings and Sunday morning and evening as required, earned extra money by baby-sitting and acquired the label from classmates of "square." I was supported by the faculty, our housemother, and those who gave me work to encourage me to "keep going." I lived with quiet joy being me without pressure to engage what others chose to do. I was not alone or lonely during college. The Presence of God was always with me. During those days I would not have called this Presence God, I would have said I had "strange feelings."

Becoming a nurse opened doors for growth over the next 40 years of my professional life. I excelled in my first job and failed in my second, and yet, God guided my way to becoming the first black head nurse in the elite, Ivy League Hospital of the University of Pennsylvania (HUP). I was hired by Julia Talmadge, who told me years later, "I hired you to fail. I was wrong. I am sorry."

> *"For I know the plans I have for you," declares the Lord, "plans to prosper you and not to harm you, plans to give you hope and a future."*
>
> Jeremiah 29:11 (INIV)

I did not fail at HUP even as I worked daily in an environment of racism, which challenged my professional attributes, placed me at personal risk and disrespected my personhood during the first 15 years of my 28 years of service. My life in HUP was sustained by the prayers of my Monumental Baptist Church family, whose pride in my accomplishments were substantial. Amidst the evils in HUP, God placed men like the late Dr. Arnold (Bud) Relman, then Chairman of the Department of Medicine in the School of Medicine of the University of Pennsylvania, and the late Mark S. Levitan, newly appointed Chief Executive Officer of HUP, in my life. They were not concerned by the color of my skin, of my being a nurse or a woman, but they recognized my abilities and the strength of being myself. People spoke of me, especially when I was not present, in ways that were not true, but knowing who I am kept me from being defined by or attached to the definitions made by others.

Mark told me years after he and I had worked together that Bud had been the force that led him and the late Dr. Thomas Langfitt to appoint me strategist for the divestiture of Graduate Hospital from the University of Pennsylvania. At the time of this appointment, I had no idea what divestiture meant. With grace and personalized attention, Mark made sure I learned. He was a certified public accountant (CPA) and, personally taught me the finance of hospitals, then sent me to advance programs at Yale, MIT, Georgetown University and the University of Michigan, which enhanced my knowledge and effectiveness as a leader. He told me more than once that he and Tom had based their decisions on "your mind, quietness of spirit, and strength of who you are." While Mark's words were true, I knew that this promotion was the result of Dottie Clark and me praying for a change from nursing supervision to "something else."

Mark and I planned and secured financing for a multi-million dollar renovation and new construction of HUP's 12 building complex. I utilized my nursing knowledge and the experiences I developed with industrial engineers, system designers, and architects about program space. In collaboration with the Medical School faculty of the University of Pennsylvania and the architects, the new construction of the Silverstein and Founders Buildings was completed. We developed a strategy for the Rhodes Building, although I retired before this building was financed and constructed. Simultaneously, I planned, led, and oversaw the completion of the renovations and additions of the Dulles, Gates and Maloney buildings of the HUP facilities. I have been amazed that I could not read a blueprint when this major redesign of HUP began. Ralph Murphy, a colleague, taught me how to read blueprints, and Mr. Robert Geddes taught me design. In this work, God revealed His love through the placement of people, without any consultation from me. I only had to comply with the nudges in my spirit.

In time, I became the Chief Operating Officer of HUP and successfully managed the operations of an almost $300 million expense budget for eight years. At the beginning of this most challenging and successful time of my career, I was not educated for any of this work, yet God led and guided me with help from many others, and I did well. What appeared to others like intellect was God in my spirit.

James, my husband, believed that God brought me to HUP to "change the plight of many." Having an open mind to newness, trusting God, and supported by James and Aunt Remell, with almost no thought about me or where I was headed, I was prepared for the work. I advanced through spiritual discernment. I knew very little about the work I had undertaken. Prayers, solitude and Scripture kept my mind stable and focused. God placed others whose genuine interest taught and guided my way. Many times others commented on my being" bright," in fact, my external work came from a guided inner spirit.

Preparation

God has used every opportunity to teach me and to prepare me for His work. The New Testament Gospels teach that before Christ began His public ministry He prepared, first with baptism and then 40 days in the wilderness where He was tested by the devil. Purposeful outcomes require preparation. Just as I had to study and practice to become a proficient practitioner of nursing, a strategist for organizations, and a leader of change in both, I had to prepare to gain access to the Power beyond my own. To become a follower of Christ required me to study the Scriptures, to live a life of love sometimes when I would have chosen not to, and to serve others before myself. I had to grow in understanding the differences between human power and spiritual power. I had to choose which would set the pattern for my life practices. I had to accept guidance, to give up control I perceived I had, and most importantly, I had to fully embrace my authentic self.

The Bible makes clear the wisdom of a Spirit-led life and a natural life. 1 Corinthians 4:20 (NLT), "The kingdom of God is not just fancy talk; it is living by God's Power." My spiritual life strengthened and merged with my natural life as I experienced biblical wisdom. Sermons, commentaries, and the voices of other believers moved me to lose interest in matters I enjoyed before, and I completely changed the sources I took into my spirit. Praying strengthened my intimacy with God. Like Momma, I pray about everything. Praying is breathing. When not talking with a person, I talk and listen to God. Listening to that quiet, inner voice, opens a Power beyond me, expanding understanding through discernment, and enhanced knowledge. I also gain wisdom about how to live and to serve.

Human Power

Human power is transient, usually acquired by military force or political power based in partisan views, professional position, social influence, financial wealth, and even bullying personalities. While any of these sources of power may give a person a definition of themselves, these powers will not last forever. In my long life, I have been saddened for friends whose worth and significance was vested in human power. When the source was diminished or was lost, so was their personal self-worth. Nothing is sadder than retired executives choosing to become consultants in the same place they may have led, holding on to what they no longer have responsibility to lead. A decision to hold on to that which validated their person can lead to depression, illness or even death. I experienced the deaths of three persons, two of them pastors of churches and one a colleague, whose lives were defined by human sources of power. Self-definition based on human power is a trap, perhaps even a pathway, to spiritual disparity.

A colleague many years ago told me this: "Organizations don't have souls, only people do. Don't let this administrative power define you, because it does not last." Bob Stein's words have never left me and his wisdom is true. Human power can be heard in the voices of those who take ownership with comments such as "my staff," "my office," "my job," "my people." These self-acclaimed powers, while not wrong, are always short-term, embedded in perceived organizational ownership rather than self-worth. As humans, we can enjoy control, perceived power, and the celebration of position, but with limited balance, human power is not sustainable.

Work, as important or as valuable as it may be, does not last forever, nor does it give sustained joy. Personally, I like working. I may even look like a workaholic, but it is not a reason for my being. Work for me is service to others, to family and friends, to community, to organizations, to schools, to the church. Doing work as service, compensated or not, provides joy. Work does not define, giving to others does, and that comes from spiritual power.

Spiritual Power

Spiritual power is less valued than human power by many because some do not understand its force. Spirit works in unexpected and unknown ways. Those of us who seek God's Power know the Source to be supernaturally revealed, and can best be seen through the eyes of faith.

My faith has grown as I live into the Scriptures. I have not had to have giant sized faith, only a little. "I tell you the truth, if you had faith even as small as a mustard seed you could say to this mountain 'Move from here to there', and it would move. Nothing could be impossible." Matthew 17:20 (NLT)

There is no risk in trusting God no matter what is before us. The Bible illuminates faith. "The fundamental fact of existence is that this trust in God, this faith, is the firm foundation under everything that makes life worth living. It's our handle on what we can't see. The act of faith distinguished our ancestors, set them above the crowd." Hebrews 11:1-2 (The Message)

Like Solomon, I seek God for wisdom. Knowledge is not wisdom, even as it includes experience, information, expertise, and so on. Choosing to ask God for wisdom as Solomon did gives access to spiritual power.

> *"Now, LORD my God, you have made your servant king in place of my father David. But I am only a little child and do not know how to carry out my duties. Your servant is here among the people you have chosen, a great people, too numerous to count or number. So give your servant a discerning heart to govern your people and to distinguish between right and wrong. For who is able to govern this great people of yours?"*
>
> *The Lord was pleased that Solomon had asked for this. So God said to him, "Since you have asked for this and not for long life or wealth for yourself, nor have asked for the death of your enemies but for discernment in administering justice, I will do what you have asked. I will give you a wise*

and discerning heart, so that there will never have been anyone like you, nor will there ever be."

1 Kings 3:7-12 (NIV)

The Apostle Paul, an educated man, in his writings of 1 Corinthians 1:19-21, 25-27, and 3:19-20 reminded Christians that wisdom is from God and may look foolish to those who do not believe. Paul, like me, had to reach a point in life where all learnings were insignificant compared with the true wisdom from God.

For it is written: "I will destroy the wisdom of the wise; the intelligence of the intelligent I will frustrate."

I Corinthians 1:19 (INIV)

God's Transforming Love

The character of God is love. He does not speak in ways we think He should. He reveals Himself when and how He chooses. God got my undivided attention when I was 24 years old, something He would do many, many more times in the pursuing years. I perceived a professional failure, which God used to teach me the first of many transitions. I took a job based on pride driven by an overly high opinion of my nursing practice, which was not validated by experience. I engaged this position believing I could do what I was not prepared for and I failed miserably. This failure defined how I would serve the rest of my life, not just professionally but in everything. After 18 months in this position living with fear and insecurity, I resigned. My narrow view of professional advancement led to my downfall. God designed this as a teaching moment and put me in a transition that forever changed my inner self. It was the beginning of my experiencing how God's love works.

Transition can be and often is transformative—a time to stop, wait and listen. Just as we pause at the fork of a road, waiting before we drive off, transition gives us times to wait. It gives us opportunity to change direction and to look within. In my first of many painful transitions of sadness, disappointment, doubt and what I viewed as failure, God taught me I could not be the decision maker. He is. I mistakenly believed God was ashamed of my behavior, my choosing to become analytical and leaning into my intellect, which was at that time an idol. God did not leave me. Instead, He surprised me by leading me back home. I had determined when I left Jacksonville, Florida, to attend college, not to return there to live but only to visit my parents or for emergencies. God led me back to York Street, that same wood-frame house where I had been formed, to teach me how to begin anew. In this place of nurture and love with my parents, my transition became an example of God's love. He transformed my life. I became a new creature. Losing pride, I became trustful in and of God and thankful in so many ways it would take many books to describe.

And I will lead the blind in a way that they know not, in paths that they have not known I will guide them. I will turn the darkness before them into light, the rough places into level ground. These are the things I will do, and I will not forsake them.

Isaiah 42:16 (RSV)

One afternoon, Momma and I were sitting on the porch of her home. A large black car stopped at our gate and a plump, spirited woman got out asking as she walked to the porch, "Is this the Flynn's home?" This woman looked so much like Momma she had to be related, and she was. Aunt Remell and Momma had not seen in each other for close to three decades. I never learned why. Aunt Remell, who lived in Philadelphia, arrived to visit her younger sister unannounced, saying, "The Spirit sent me." Her visit, she said, was "spontaneous. I felt it in my spirit and I came." I had only known Aunt Remell through family stories. This was the first time we were meeting each other. During her visit of several days, my beloved Aunt became a Divine gift - an angel sent by God. Her visit began my spiritual transformation from "thinking more highly of myself than I should have" to a new spirit.

There are many stories in the Bible that validate angels, beings bringing messages from God for protection and comfort. "There is joy in the presence of God's angels when even one sinner repents." Luke 15:10 (NLT). I spent hours talking/confessing to Aunt Remell, lamenting how I had allowed pride to overtake my common sense. Instead of scolding me, Aunt Remell invited me to Philadelphia "to find a job," and to "get a husband." Her statements, which appeared to be "off," were in fact prophetic. I came to Philadelphia and I got a job at the Hospital of the University of Pennsylvania. I met and married James, leading to the best relationship of my life after God. Each time I reflect on this miraculous period in my life, I know without a doubt that my view is too narrow to see the horizons of possibilities. God sent Aunt Remell to Florida to reconcile with her sister and, I got a huge bonus - God's forgiveness and a future.

When I arrived in Philadelphia on a dark cloudy day a month after my Aunt's visit to Florida, I thought this journey was a mistake. I arrived at her home on 427 North 33rd Street. She was not at home. I mistakenly thought she had forgotten she had invited me. She had not. Virgie, a woman who assisted Aunt Remell, told me "she had gone around the corner to take her shoes to the shop." Aunt Remell gave me a room in the large rooming house she operated for fragile adults. Interestingly, my transformation came when I was mature enough to receive its wisdom and the gift of discernment to help me know the difference between human power and spiritual, supernatural Power.

About a week after I arrived in Philadelphia, I learned that Aunt Remell's trip around the corner the day of my arrival at her door was to visit and to tell James Brisbon I was coming that day. Between the time of my Aunt's visit to Florida and her return to Philadelphia, she had decided James would be my husband. A few weeks later one morning as I helped Virgie clean up from breakfast, Aunt Remell called me to the front window of her home to tell me the man walking past was my husband. James and I married a year later and lived in a harmonious relationship for close to five decades.

> *See, I am doing a new thing! Now it springs up; do you not perceive it?*
>
> Isaiah 43:19 (INIV)

Security, confidence, peace and contentment comes from God. I became proficient in the many professional aspects of life through study and experiences. I have grown intimate with God by studying His words and trusting Him in faith. I no longer seek to hear God audibly although I often do hear Him in the voices of other human beings. Intimacy with God resides in my spirit with full access to the wisdom He provides. This intimate relationship does not shield me from temptations but it does keep me from indulging. In my deepest desire to know God better, I make a deliberate choice to seek Him first. I am no longer distracted by the trivial. Peace is the gift I receive for seeking Him first in all things. And He continues to give me relationships and communities in which I can serve.

Relationships

Relationships are critical to spiritual health. The key is communication with God and others. The more I talk with God the closer I grow to him. I am able to recognize His hand in situations, to hear His voice and rest in His decisions, giving thanks to Him for all His benefits.

I acknowledge this discipline is not a walk in the park, romantic, debatable or a topic to be used as show and tell. Simply, this discipline is a singular, focused intimacy with God. An intimate relationship with God is to give Him control of our will and to ask for His help. He will grow the effective human relationships.

When I was eighty years old, I celebrated a grand birthday. As I pondered this time in my life, I asked God "What's next?" My life was full but I could not discern if I was done. I had been a widow nine years; fortunate to have my adult children Edgar and Nancy living close by with grandchildren Emerson, Abby, Welton, and Mitchell. My life was enriched by special, loving, close relationships with Bret (Perkins), a son I did not give birth to, along with his wife Donna and sons Tieran and Tazio. I was blessed with daughter relationships with Lynette (Brown-Sow) and Mary (Tutt Garrett). I was teaching Bible to seniors (older than me), and to the women of the "Gathering" – Toni (Styer), Jackie (Allen), Ernestine (Estes), Earline (Williams), Regina (Wade), Maxine (Tucker), and Francene (Brown). I spent every first Friday of the month with Paula (Gross), my sister in ordination as Elders of the church. I am often called upon to share the life of others as mentor with Tracy (Pou), Dixie (James), and Rosie (Hsueh). My life of relationships was indeed broad, authentic and rich.

Responding to my "what's next" was a call from Amy Kardash, then program Director and now President of the In Trust Center for Theological Schools with a question, "Could I assist Dr. Vergel Lattimore, newly appointed President of Hood Theological School in Salisbury, North Carolina, with a Board of Trustees Retreat?" I did not know Dr. Lattimore, but was familiar with his school. I did have a decade relationship with Amy and felt called to respond. And I did respond, leading to a broader network of rich, spiritual relationship, which I could not have imagined.

There is no risk in following or asking God, "What's next?" As Chambers said, "God does not tell us what He will do, He reveals Himself to us." Writing this chapter at 85 years old, I thank God for the discipline, gifts and wisdom He has chosen to give me to serve Him. In the last five years, God has given me physical strength to travel to and collaborate in spiritual discernment to build and develop relationships with leaders, preparing others for the Church. Across a year, I visited with leaders on the site of a school, in a Philadelphia conference room, or in my home. God has used the wisdom that He has given me for His purposes, not in a museum but in a living stream. This stream continues to flow through mutual, loving and respectful relationships begun with Dr. Vergel Lattimore and expanded to include: Dr. Alton B. Pollard, President of Louisville Presbyterian Seminary; Dr. Edward Wheeler, President of the Interdenominational Theological Center in Atlanta, Georgia; Dr. Michael Brown, President of Payne Theological Seminary; Dr. Johnny Hill, Dean of Shaw School of Divinity Shaw University, Dr. Paulette Dillard, President of Shaw University, and Dr. Corey Walker, prior Executive Vice President of Samuel Dewitt Proctor School of Theology at Virginia Union University. Relationships with these leaders and those they lead have expanded my relationships by asking God for direction.

In responding to my feasible request of "what's next?" God gave me the transformative gift of wisdom through exposure and friendship with Dr. John Kinney who served the School of Theology at Virginia Union for more than two decades. My relationship with John Kinney and theological leaders soared, not from aspects of theological issues but because of wisdom from God.

> *Do nothing from selfishness or conceit, but in humility count others better than yourselves.*
>
> Philippians 2:3 (RSV)

TWO

The Wisdom from Prayer

Tell God what you need and thank Him for all He has done. If you do this, you will experience God's peace, which is far more wonderful than the human mind can understand.

Philippians 4:6b, 7a (NLT)

Praying is not a natural behavior. In fact, prayer is counter-intuitive to our human self. If people pray at all, it is likely to be in times of stress, pain or disasters. Churches fill up after major tragedies and multiple requests are made for prayer. Some include the persons who report the news. Even so, when prayers are offered, God hears. It seems many believe in God but not enough to talk to Him regularly, which is what prayer is. A significant number of people, including Christians, choose to seek answers to concerns from the internet, tapes, television, experience, books, friends, even psychiatrists. There is no doubt these sources will give information, but none can give wisdom. The only source of wisdom is God, who can only be accessed in prayer, even as He is omnipresent (everywhere).

My history of prayer has shaped me in a way that I cannot live without talking to God, although I cannot see Him. Praying is the foundation of my faith, the fuel that has taken me through and into a privileged life. I am not sure if I can live without prayer, but I will never know. I will not take the risk. I talk to God quite a lot—it's the most valuable gift I give to myself every day. Talking with God opens pathways to understanding myself, others, and the world in which I live. Prayer is the way to wisdom. Many of us believe we know God, even as we think we know what to do, where to go and what will happen, so why pray? We pray out of need. We really don't have answers to our questions. We lack recognition of the source of our intellect that forms what we think we know. We value our intellect, the news, our education, our positions and personal perceived power more than the power of the Divine Being.

Prayer is to cultivate, maintain, and grow in intimacy with God. Cultivating an intimate relationship with God is greater than, yet similar to, that which we develop with those closest to us. I talk to my children, Edgar and Nancy, almost every day, sometimes more than once. They are my closest intimate friends, our relationship developed over their lives through talking. We don't talk to get things from each other, rather to stay closely related as our lives change even in a day. Praying to God is the same, but much, much greater, because talking with God enhances all my conversations including those with my children and others I encounter across a day.

God is a Spirit. He cannot be seen or touched, only experienced in our inner spirit; this is the connection of prayer. While prayer does not change things, it does change us. Prayer has changed my perspective in matters of family, work, and community, which guide my actions, not just for myself, but for others as well. Knowing the character of God of the Bible strengthens my praying. God is love; prayer then must have love as its foundation.

Prayer is not to cover all our bases. God already knows everything. He is all-knowing, and knows more about our bases than we know. Talking with God is to gain understanding and wisdom about how to respond to the realities of the day, to align my will with the will of God. David, credited with writing the major parts of the Psalms, says

> *Before a word is on my tongue you know it completely, O Lord.*
>
> Psalm 139: 4 (NIV)

We pray to build intimacy, to empty our spirits of those matters which capture us; to share our concerns for family, friends, the church and community; to give thanks for what we have been given; to thank God for being who He is; to accept what He knows will come that we don't want. In fact, genuine prayer talks to God about everything; however, we cannot tell Him what to do or when to act.

The writer of Proverbs, a Book of Wisdom in the Bible teaches:

> *Start with God, the first step in learning by bowing down to him; only fools thumb their noses at such wisdom of learning.*
>
> (Proverbs 1:7) *The Message*

It does not matter whether I stumble over words, stammer or groan. I may not even know what to say. Prayer is not a performance, but is a matter of the heart. God listens, He hears what I (we) say because our hearts are important to Him. I cannot bargain with God, coerce or direct Him. In this intimate relationship, God runs the show, not me. I pray with honesty, not holding anything back, free of doubt, and with an attitude of reverence. The wonderful thing about prayer is that it can be done privately, publicly, any hour of the day or night and, anywhere. There is no voicemail, no delay, call back messages or typing. Only my open heart connecting with Divine Spirit for as long as I need. My conversation may be short, one word, long, or not uttered. Praying is what I do; response is what God does.

I have prayed short prayers many times over my life. I recall a prayer during such a time that has been answered over and over again. When Nancy was four years old, Dr. Rita Weton diagnosed our daughter with a deficiency that had possibilities of damaging her growth. Rita ordered medication for us to give Nancy nightly. After the first dose of this medicine, Nancy did not want to have anything to do with it because of the taste. Her tears were heart breaking. Edgar would lovingly hold Nancy in his arms, as either James or I would attempt to give her this bitter medicine. Our nightly task seemed like torture to this precious little girl. One night I said, through tears, "Lord, take care of my baby." That night, I stopped giving Nancy the medicine.

Today Nancy is over 50 years old, a family medicine physician, a loving mother and a daughter only God could have made. God has and still does "take care of my baby." I had forgotten those times until I looked back and again thanked God for Nancy as she sat with me, patiently placing an order on the internet. I was reminded once again to pray in the minute, a frequent practice. When someone asks me to pray for them, I pray right then. I pray when I see or hear things that make me sad, at the bedside of friends, for colleagues traveling. These are often short prayers, but I know they are heard. The wisdom of prayer tells me so.

God is a God of surprises. Some years ago, I assisted Pinn Memorial Baptist Church in Philadelphia, Pennsylvania, with the realignment of their ministries. Dr. Jacob Chatman always ended his prayer with "surprise us God." I was reminded during these times of prayer of the many situations when God indeed did surprise me. I now have adopted his words in my own prayers. Before I developed the intimacy with God I now enjoy, I depended on my skills, strategic thought, intellect, and analysis for answers. While these gifts often worked, I can attest that prayer always worked, more so when joined by or in a community. The key to receiving answers from God is belief and trust, which is a matter of faith.

In late 1978, 20 years after I began work as head nurse in Neurology at the Hospital of the University of Pennsylvania (HUP), I was named Chief Operating Officer of the Hospital. This was a time when racial hate, prejudices and discrimination against women, especially one who could not be bought, was not so much verbally stated, but worked to sabotage my leadership in any way possible. While much of the ugly, petty ways in the HUP environment are a distant memory, some remain vivid as I recall the wisdom of prayer.

In 1982, it was evident I was changing the culture in HUP for workers, especially the support staff who, for years, had not been heard as much as they were seen or "patted on the head." In consultation with the Chief Executive Officer, the late Mark S. Levitan, I restructured the Human Resource Department. This restructuring established a system of counselors to address specific issues of the staff, ensured that compensations were equal or above other hospitals in the city, and created a bonus reward for perfect attendance. We conducted quarterly town halls where people could come and tell me what was on their minds. Imagine my dismay when I learned that there was an effort to unionize the workers. I am not anti-union. I believed that working conditions in an institution are the responsibility of leadership, and workers should not have to pay a fee to be valued and compensated. I could not understand the reason this organizing was underway.

I talked with the late Rev. M.M. Peace, my Pastor. His advice was to pray, and he said, "I will pray with and for you." Frankly, at the time I was not sure what prayer would do. After all, we had hired consultants to examine our policies, the work environment, authorized surveys, and trained supervisors. I had also authorized a new position for the Human Resource Department to hire a workplace counselor. I was more than a little concerned that a union at HUP would be an issue with the University of Pennsylvania's administration and represent a blemish against me. The support staff at that time was made up of 90% black people, as am I. How, I asked myself, could this be? All the consultants reported they could not "find cause for labor unrest."

The candidate vetted for appointment to the new position in the Human Resource Department was scheduled to see me the day before the employees were to vote "yes" or "no" for a union. As a matter of policy, I reserved the right to have final approval for persons working directly with staff. The young man recommended for this position arrived promptly for our conversation. He was well dressed, spoke articulately, and had a pleasant manner. He met every specified professional qualification, and yet I had an overwhelming negative response to his presence. I felt a bit crazy, as I experienced a feeling of impending doom. The man did not look threatening.

I did not approve the hire. When the Director of Human Resources asked why, I said "my gut." A few days later, the Director resigned. He never said why and did not seem angry. I later learned both he and the candidate leaned favorably toward unionization, and were intending to benefit from the success of a "yes" vote. The employees did not vote for unionization then and have not since. God does surprise, He does not tell me what He will do, He responds with revelation. The outcome of this very troubling event was a revelation of the wisdom of prayer, those of Rev. Peace, and many others who prayed.

Prayer is not fancy talk. Prayer is a biblical truth. Answers to prayers are God's call, His decision. My part is to ask, wait and follow. The Bible instructs me how in Hebrew 4:16 (NLT).

> *Let us come boldly to the throne of our gracious God. There we will receive His mercy and grace to help us when we need it.*

I have been guilty of praying with flawed knowledge, misconceptions, even with entitlement and pride. In 1987, my husband, James, was diagnosed with Alzheimer's Disease. I asked God to heal him, even though I knew medically that would be unlikely. My prayer was out of a prideful spirit. I reasoned that James was a good man, a devoted and supported husband, loving father and a deacon in the church. Surely, God will make James better. I had to learn works are done out of a grateful heart, not as a reward. My thought of God's "no" became entrenched in my heart, anger and rage became my silent fight. I behaved normally, but was far from being a person of prayer. As James' condition continued to grow worse, I went into total denial for six years. The stress pretense and misconceptions disrupted the blood flow in my brain. I had a stroke.

I was hospitalized for two days. My neurological system was thoroughly tested. The stroke was real, the cause was not as clear. The medical determination was "stress and denial." I went home from the hospital with instructions from Dr. Steven Galetta, to "rest, decrease stress, take a baby aspirin and return to see me in a month." Devastated, I left the hospital concerned that the next stroke could be more damaging. My stroke left me with a weakened right side, but my brain was left intact.

I sat at home crying for several days with seemingly only self-talk. The God I expected to heal James did not respond. Prayer did not come easily, nor did I know what to pray for. I experienced guilt, tons of heart-to-heart with myself and questions. "What will we do?" I pondered, James is ill and so am I. I had forgotten my history of wisdom from prayer, and turned to self.

> *Sometimes our own actions put us in dungeons, and things beyond our control is the reason. But however we get there,*

we cannot get out.

Then God comes and rescues us.

Eugene Peterson, *Praying with the Psalms*

I had placed myself in a dungeon. I felt I deserved better, however, God said, "No!" As I sat pondering, "What next," my brother Welton called. He asked what was going on with me. Welton, who lived in California, had been called by my brothers Willie and Milton, who lived in Florida, to say I had lost my sight. I did lose my sight for a few minutes, it signaled the beginning of my stroke; but my sight was restored shortly after swallowing two aspirins.

I told my brother the plan for me. He asked, "Can you fly?" I said, "I think so but will ask my doctor." After I got the OK to fly, James and I boarded a United Airlines flight to Los Angeles, California, where Welton met us at the airport. He took us to a full-service condominium in Orange County, several blocks from the Crystal Cathedral. I have never known why Welton chose this location but it became my place of healing.

This condo had a balcony, about the only thing I can remember about this place. The balcony overlooked a small well-manicured garden of beautiful grass with yellow and red flowers around the borders. This view remains embedded in my mind almost 25 years later. I cannot remember how many days I sat looking at this garden, weak, tearful, and afraid for our future. I do remember overwhelming feelings of helplessness. My prayers, if at all, were quiet groaning. I don't remember praying. I cried myself empty to a place of dryness and gave up my thoughts, which had become useless. Oswald Chambers says, "We can only truly find God when we give up ourselves."

One morning as I sat on the balcony, silently listening, my body experienced an embodied warmth as if I was being cuddled closely. I was very frightened. I thought, "I am having a stroke." I was not. Gradually the warmth dissipated. A lightness overwhelmed my entire being the likes of which I have not experienced since. I did not see or hear anything, just felt a sense of peace.

> *The Spirit helps us in our weakness. We do not know what we ought to pray for, but the Spirit himself intercedes for us with groans that words cannot express.*
>
> Romans 8:26 (NIV)

This was a Biblical truth for me, that long-ago day, when I could not pray.

We returned to Philadelphia from Los Angeles a couple of weeks later. James still had advancing Alzheimer's Disease and I still had a damaged brain, but prayer had changed me. For the next 11 years, prayer was my lifeline. My dark years were lighted with and by conversations with God about everything: honest and steadfast, many long, teary prayers, some with one word, "Jesus" or "help," and other prayers were "Lord, I need you." I received answers for every prayer, timely enough and sometimes surprising.

Among the most memorable answers of the short prayers came as a surprise in 1996. I was late leaving home to attend a Board of Trustees meeting at the Community College of Philadelphia, sixteen blocks from our Baring Street home. I had sold our car in early May in preparation for moving to a condominium in August. Our home, at the northwest corner of 33rd and Baring Streets, was not a location for cabs. A block west, at 34th and Baring Streets, offered better options and was where I intended to go. As I locked the door of our house, I said aloud, sorta' to the air, "I need a ride."

Before I reached the gate of our house, a cab traveling east stopped at the corner, James Davis the driver asked, "Do you need a cab?" Surprised, I said, "I do." As I got in the car, Jake, as he became known to us said, "I don't usually drive this street, but something told me to turn off 34th Street and come this way." Jake, from that day in 1996, until his vision became compromised in 2011, was the Brisbon family's driver. For me, it was not a coincidence rather a Divine response to prayer, even one that was half- hearted, and a Biblical truth.

Isaiah 65:24 (NIV) teaches, "I will answer them before they even call to me. While they are still talking to me about their need I will go ahead and answer their prayer."

James died November 12, 2004. Surviving living alone these last thirteen years has been challenging at times, but my talking, friendship and intimacy with God continues to grow. Praying is now like breathing for me. In 2005, I was led to join the First Presbyterian Church in Philadelphia. I was ordained Elder in 2006. This community has given me companionship I had not expected. In recent years, I joined the deacons after church each Sunday to pray for others. Jesus teaches us to pray for others.

On February 12, 2013, I reached 80 years old. Not quite ready to stop contributing, I asked God "What next?" He responded through a call from Amy Kardash, then Director of Program, now President of the In Trust Center for Theological Education. Amy asked if I would accept an engagement at Hood Seminary in Salisbury, North Carolina. I said yes. In the last five years, God has guided me to travel several times a month with focused intentionality and joy. God reminds me that He called Moses at 80 years to lead the Israelites out of Egypt. My assignment is to share the wisdom God gives me, not to be concerned about my age.

> *Retire inwardly, wait to feel God's spirit, discovering and moving away that which is contrary to His Holy nature and leading into that which is acceptable to God. As our minds are joined to God in prayer, true light is received.*
>
> J. Pennington (1617-1679)

I center my mind on God every morning, sometimes before I get out of bed. My time alone with God shows up in my outer expression of confidence as I go about what is before me. I am clear that I don't know how to face the day unless I hear from God, and I want to.

Very early in the morning while it was still dark, Jesus got

> *up, left the house and went off to a solitary place where He prayed.*
>
> Mark 1:35

My solitary place is a large chair in my bedroom, early every morning. I get a large cup of coffee, a tall glass of water and talk with God. I listen for His voice in my spirit with focus, conscious not to allow distractions. Years of prayer have taught me that focus is critical, as the other voice (my natural one) will strive to be dominant.

The Bible has taught me how to pray.

> *When you pray, go into your room, close the door and pray to your Father, who is unseen.*
>
> Matthew 6:5

I close the door of my mind to the next task, appointments, and sounds in my apartment or the traffic below my condominium. Matthew goes on to say,

> *Then your Father, who sees what is done in secret will reward you.*

I don't interpret reward as instant gratification, rather an answer to petitions or requests to God in my prayers as I move along. On some days before I leave the chair, I receive an answer; other times, it is days later and sometimes even now, not yet.

Matthew continues on to say (vs 7).

> *When you pray, do not keep on babbling.*

Matthew writes the inspired words of God as he records how Jesus taught us to pray. Confessing wrongs I have done, no matter how small or large they may be, seeking forgiveness so that pathways are opened. This kind of prayer has humbled me and made me accept my part in events, and clearing my mind with God in private makes me better in public.

For those who may be reading this book and do not pray, I encourage you to begin. Ask and God answers. Even J. Edgar Hoover, not a popular person with many people including me, said, "Prayer is man's greatest means of tapping the infinite resources of God."

Prayer is the entry-way to God's wisdom. Open your heart to Him and receive a free gift, one that will lead to peace.

THREE

The Wisdom of Being Yourself

You are blessed when you are content with just who you are - no more, no less. That's the moment you find yourselves proud owners of everything that can't be bought.

Matthew 5:5 (*The Message)*

When we use what we have been given, we make our best contributions. Many people spend significant time trying to be who they are not, without recognizing what an incredible burden it is to attempt to be someone else. We wear ourselves out, becoming frustrated seeking positions professionally or socially, striving for physical beauty, attempting to achieve perfect bodies, working too much or too long, or trying to become rich in unattainable situations. Dressing like others, competing with others, even attaching oneself to another person is a loud message saying, "I don't like me." A lack of self-awareness drives unrealistic goals to be who you are not. Sadly, this lack of recognition, or an understanding that striving to be who we cannot be, becomes an addiction. We are important contributors to humanity, not because of what we do, rather because of who we are. How many times do we introduce ourselves by the title of a position? It is a rarity to hear someone say, "I am Betty," instead of, "I am the Commissioner" of something or the executive of an organization. Introducing oneself by title seems to give more status than our name. This type of self-identification becomes problematic when the titles are no longer in place.

The lack of self-awareness of personal value can become a trap that sets behavior and patterns that can be embraced as truth, leading to disillusionment, disappointments, pain, and in some instances, despair.

We are loved by God even if one does not believe in God. There is no better knowledge than to know God loves us even if no one else loves us, and we only have to be ourselves. Accepting the love freely given by God removes what my friend David Black calls "a hole in the soul." Trying to fill "a hole in the soul" often leads to seeking approval from others, insecurity, comparison with others, accepting or placing oneself in a vulnerable position, or sometimes, even, being in harm's way. A theologian once told me "many of us have been complicit in giving up who we are to become who we will never be." Both David and my theologian friend are persons of wisdom living magnificently, modeling and teaching others, and have achieved in their professional and vocational lives simply by being who they are.

I admire people who have the grit to achieve their goals as long as those goals are for the good of others, not personal aggrandizing. The self-need to achieve, more likely than not, will compromise who we are. The years I supervised nurses in an intensive care unit of the Hospital of the University of Pennsylvania (HUP) was a memorable experience that taught me the danger of not knowing who we are. A nurse with exceptional skill so compromised her need for approval from doctors that she pushed peers away, worked harder than needed, and eventually became so fatigued her effectiveness was impaired. This nurse was physically attractive, married, and had much to be grateful for, but it was not enough to fill her being. She needed approval.

I had a friend who was unable to accept having been fired from a position by which she identified herself. She became ill and unhappy and destroyed relationships. She was rejected because of mean-spirited actions caused by a victim's mentality, not the work she did, which was very good. She once told me she had "never been loved" by her father. She was unwilling to accept responsibility for her actions in this job termination, instead blaming others, when in reality she was angry with a deceased father. Love is critical to our mental well-being, and when it is not experienced in human relationships, can undermine who we are and become a barrier to receiving the ultimate love from God. Acceptance of ourselves and accepting grace from God is the answer to peace.

Only by daring to be ourselves can we deeply know others.

Mark Nepo

We talk quite a lot about self-esteem, sometimes placing blame or reasons for our lack of loving ourselves or for not being authentic. The truth is, being authentic is a personal choice. Knowing who we are in God and maintaining a right relationship with breathless pursuit of the Divine Being is the choice for authenticity.

Enjoy what you have rather than desiring what you don't have.

Ecclesiastes 6:9 (NIV)

Shortly after I established Brisbon & Associates, I was invited by the late George Longshore to monitor a gathering of executive leaders. This gathering, conducted by George, a human resources expert, designed a day titled, "Finding Yourself as a Leader" to help executives better understand their leadership style, the culture established by their style, and to examine where their strengths lie in leading. Fifteen men showed up, representing banking, investments, not-for-profits, real estate and the church. A startling outcome was 12 of these men acknowledged they "could not find their leadership style because they were not sure who they really were."

Half of these men were in positions chosen by family or were married into a family to continue a legacy.

By the end of that day, these men acknowledged that a lack of enjoying their work or knowing themselves had led to unacceptable compromises, even as they kept business matters intact. Some acknowledged drinking too much, unfaithfulness, or depression, among many other confessed barriers to "finding themselves in leadership." Pleasing others, in this group, had compromised them to a point of losing personal identity and joy. George guided these men to reexamine their personal mission and to get in touch with themselves. I never knew if this work changed any of those attending. I do know three of these men resigned over the next year to "spend time in pursuit of other activities." One of these men entered seminary.

My opportunity to be included as an observer of this programmatic focus enriched me to re-assess my personal authenticity. Having the freedom to be one's self enhances gifts given, no matter the position or job. To get to this point requires an honest assessment of our motives, including why there is a feeling of lack in our inner self. When I was 9 or 10 years old, I considered myself less "pretty" than my sisters Evelyn and Barbara. Without injury to my spirit, Daddy told me, "You can be anything you want to be." He did not say anything about beauty; he simply gave me a choice to accept who I am.

Being myself grew out of Daddy's simple statement and shaped my moral compass. I had never been a "good fit" in family, early childhood development, or college, and my Dad was fine that I was not. Not fitting has led to professional success. I am a shy, tall, black woman with curly hair, and a big smile, and a good listener with a compassionate heart. I prefer to engage in small groups, even individually, which eliminates a desire to be included in many activities common to others and not enjoyed by me.

If my presence does not contribute to an outcome, small or large, I prefer not to be involved, not as judgment of others, but it is what fits who I know myself to be. A woman in my condo, for more than a year, continued to invite me to activities in which I had no interest. Recently she invited me to join a "book club." When I declined, she went on to say, "Oh come on, you will enjoy yourself." I said, "I will not, in fact, it is unlikely we read the same type books." She asked, "What do you read?" I said, "The Bible, Merton, Chambers, and Ancient Fathers." Before I could complete my sentence, she said "Oh." She has not invited me since to anything. Knowing who I am is as important as knowing who I am not.

As a supervisor of nurses between 1962 and 1974 in HUP, I chose to make rounds with the doctors, a behavior which was not common to five supervisor colleagues, an action that did not fit in the scheme of nursing supervisory behavior. I viewed rounds as the best time to hear the medical plans for patients and to integrate those decisions in nursing care. Some questioned why rounds were needed and were even critical of them, but these rounds enhanced care to patients and taught nurses. Years after I retired from HUP, my daughter Nancy and I attended an event to celebrate Dr. Jerry Johnson, a renowned geriatrician. As we left the auditorium, a woman I did not recognize walked over to us and said, "I have wanted to see you to tell you how you changed my life." Ms. Sullivan recounted an event one morning doing rounds. She went on to say that she had earned a doctorate degree and now teaches others "how to see the whole person's needs." Ms. Sullivan reminded me that as a student nurse she had prepared rigorously to present her patient to me during rounds, but had forgotten to ask a person with a limited capacity to walk about steps in their home. She said when I asked her "how many steps" were in this person's home, she was embarrassed, a lesson that led her to see people as "whole beings, not just a patient." She used this lesson to pursue a doctorate degree and to teach others. I said, "Thank you."

Nancy and I said good-bye to Ms. Sullivan, and as we approached the parking lot, my daughter said, "Do you realize what that lady just said?" I said yes. What I did not say was making rounds did not fit in a culture of leadership that I chose not to be a part of. Not fitting the model of nurse supervisor did not grow friends, in fact, many chose to participate in giving me unattractive labels.

My lack of fit as a supervisor of nursing led to effective relationships with the Medical School Faculty of the University of Pennsylvania who were purposed to give excellent service to patients. My work did not involve telling anyone what to do but led to what I agreed to do; to collaborate with doctors on how to meet our mission to patients. These relationships led first to being appointed strategist and planner for HUP and Graduate Hospital, and in a few years, I was promoted to Chief Operating Officer of HUP.

We are not at risk when we know ourselves. As we change, mature, and make choices, our life is consistent. We act from the core of who we are, not from situations or circumstances. Daddy decided I would be a nurse. I did not know what else to be. I enjoyed serving others and I practiced nursing through teaching others who were leading units, and I supervised nurses for 25 years of my professional career. I was neither unhappy nor happy as a nurse, but I knew deep in myself that I did not fit. I excelled as a nurse because excelling is what I do, who I am. I had to seek and become aware of my spiritual gifts to identify and know my strengths, which opened me to fit.

The Scriptures are rich on the matter of spiritual gifts (1 Corinthians 12, Romans 12). Spiritual gifts come from God and are different from skills or education - gifts informed by intellect. When embraced, our spiritual gifts fit and we know who we are. We are authentic. Every human being has spiritual gifts that constitute their core being. When we seek to be different, we violate that being.

My strongest spiritual gifts are wisdom, leadership, discernment, teaching, and administration. Recognizing and using our gifts allows us to overcome barriers and obstacles put in our life path. By this, I don't mean we get what we want. I do mean we get what God plans. Being who you are in private and public awakens authenticity. There is no need for facades as we are a gift to those we encounter, serve and live with, and to whom we express love. Our gifts give confidence to face what comes, sometimes even the recognition that our gifts are real. We are freed from fear, feelings of being less than or better than, allowing growth, enabling engagement in honest discourse, and removing temptations of excess, whether eating, drinking, working, talking, or seeking attention.

Acceptance and living into authenticity is living from the inside out. My gifts have been and are being used to lift others. Wisdom guides every encounter with my children, those I birthed and those chosen; grandchildren; those who call me mentor; those who call me "professional coach;" in the church; and among friends and enemies. Because I know who I am and who I am not, I can meet and accept others where they are.

Given sincerity, there will be enlightenment.

The Doctrine of The Mean, 200 BCE

FOUR

Wisdom from Marriage

Marriage is to be a lifetime plan, not something that can be conveniently disposed of in a lawyer's office and a courtroom.

J. Stephen Lang

There we were sitting in the Thunder Grill in Union Station in Washington D.C., three colleagues planning a program for theological schools, when one of my friends, almost abruptly, asked, "Delores, what is marriage?" I said, "One relationship occupied by two people." My colleague said, "Yes, like the chain is as strong as the weakest link."

I do not remember how we got to talking about marriage, but our conversation moved into what makes a relationship work for the long term. The three of us represented 140 years of marriage. We had quite a lot to say about this exclusive, intimate relationship. Each of our marriages are different but the three of us agreed getting the right partner made our relationships survive and thrive. I am a widow of a relationship that extended close to 50 years. My colleagues' spouses are alive, each having lived peacefully in marriage four decades or more. So what does it take to live reasonably comfortable in a long marriage? This reading below describes, at least for me, the best accurate meaning of marriage, and the work and commitment required to stay for the long haul. One thing that the three of us said was our spouses are our first priority after God, not a difficult task with love as the root of the relationship. Love is a transformative force and authentic marriage does not survive absent love.

> *When we enter into the covenant of marriage, it affects every aspect of our being - our time, our energy, our income, our personal space, our heart, our bodies, our relationships, our leisure, our future. Nothing is left untouched in the partnership of marriage.*
>
> (*Time Alone with God*; December 22nd reading)

Some Saturday mornings, Bret and I walk close to five miles as we discuss matters of interest to each other and many times, broader subject of politics, community or even futures. One morning as we strolled along Spruce Street, our conversation turned to marriage. Bret said, "In your next book, talk about marriage." Three years would pass before I began to write this chapter, and here is what I have to say about marriage and wisdom from a long, harmonious marriage.

Many people spend more time talking about a wedding than the truth of combining lives in an intimate, exclusive relationship. Choosing to plan the details of the marital event rather than the path of life is a mistake. While marriage can be a romantic venture and include physical attraction, these aspects alone are short-lived as they may only be experienced in the beginning. Being in love is not always loving. Marriage is not for selfish people. Discussing uncertainties, challenges and disagreements are not the language of a romanticized courtship, nor does this language grow physical attraction. The glue that holds marriage tightly interwoven and joyful is communication, honestly speaking and listening.

Talking about everything eliminates a need to explain later. Talking reduces secrets, and any matters that have the possibility, even a little, to set up barriers in our hearts, should be shared openly. Momma once told me, "There is nothing bad or good that you should keep from your husband." She and Daddy were married 66 years before she died. My parents were so closely aligned they began to look like each other physically. It was hard to see where one stopped and the other began.

Marriage is not an easy journey nor is it a statistical finding. It is not a study or observation, rather a hard-lived experience. Like all other relationships, marriage has two perspectives. However, in a marriage, both perspectives must be common, or at least there must be an agreement not to damage the whole of the partnership. Disagreements or differences in personality need not be damaging but rather accepted, And differences must not breed contempt, complaining or disrespectful and disruptive behavior. Talking and listening is the path to reduce, if not eliminate, questions, speculations, uncertainty, assumptions, misunderstandings, suspicions, and misguided thinking. Communication is the hard work of marriage.

Accepting Differences

James and I were distinctly different. We loved the person we met. We did not try to change each other although we had many conversations about those things that create barriers. James was grounded, quiet, stubborn, and thoughtful. At the time we married, I was less settled. We had different personal interests; he, sports, while I preferred reading and music. Even so, he enjoyed jazz; me, classical instruments. Our reading content differed. James enjoyed newspapers and magazines; I preferred novels, autobiographies, and the Bible. Our values of money management, sex, family responsibilities, church worship, helping others, and children, including how many, were perfectly matched. Despite aligned values, we did not agree on some things. James did not want me to work. I knew I had to and had we not worked out an acceptance, we would not have been able to marry. Working for me was more of a social and an intellectual engagement and gave me personal interdependence, which I needed, even as I loved James. We had to talk about what work meant to my spiritual health and how to navigate his pride.

Beginning a courtship and marriage with open, honest conversation for as long as it takes, even at the risk of delaying the legal ceremony is wise. It is unlikely that either partner will change significantly in marriage. James and I got to know each other before we knew we would be husband and wife. We discussed our past experiences, family culture, parents, work, children, faith and church participation. James was not 'high' on the church, I was. He did not believe in divorce, I did. At 35 years old, when we were introduced by my maternal Aunt Remelle, James was not a stranger to relationships with other women. A handsome guy, he enjoyed the attention of women who were attracted to him. In fact, until he met me, he said, "I don't plan to marry." Witnessing friends' negative experiences with marriage made him less attracted to a marital union. Getting to know me in many long conversations sitting on the steps of Aunt Remelle's home changed his mind about marriage. We knew each other's warts and acknowledged they were there. I would say we had an on-boarding process that only had two players - James and me. The exclusionary effect of the beginning years of our marriage stayed in place for the life of our marriage.

Family Culture

Marriage is to the person we chose, but we also marry our families. Family culture does matter. Being formed in a culture will generally influence how we live as adults, much so in our marriage. The marriage of our parents influenced our own, positively and negatively. Before saying "I do," it is a good idea to know family cultures as more often than not our family culture will influence our marital culture. In-law engagement can and has been problematic in some marriages. When there is conflict with parents, expectations from either partner can be emotionally torn. There is no shortage of parents who don't like the person their child may have chosen to marry. Unresolved conflict or lack of clarity is likely to be a barrier between partners, and it does not go away.

My husband was reared by a strong domineering mother and an absent father who spent time traveling as a preacher. Rev. James Brisbon, Sr. died in James' early adulthood .The Brisbon family culture of three siblings, practiced the Pentecostal faith and, while not rich, was stable financially. James' mother owned properties that gave the family a comfortable income. His mother did not like me. My Flynn family culture of eight siblings lived in an intact parental relationship, practiced the Baptist tradition, and we were poor. My Dad accepted those we chose to marry; Momma generally did not, even though James became her favorite son-in-law. Knowing and understanding our family's dynamics guided us with in-law engagement. It would have been disruptive to our relationship had I not known been told by James how his mother behaved, creating a barrier between he and I. Talking honestly about our parents and their marital culture led to an accepting posture which did not become an issue to our relationship. We had to know from each other not so much what our parents expected but what we expected from ourselves. Our talking and being realistic about our family cultures eliminated intrusion or violating our genetic family culture, as we set standards for our own relationship. These early conversations determined where we would spend holidays, vacations, visits and who would or would not take care of our children.

While we sought to respect our family cultures, we recognized some aspects could not be a part of our own. We navigated these differences in honest conversation, accepting some things we could not change and determined that our desire to live with each other and, yes, our need for each other, would be a priority. It worked.

> *A man leaves his father and mother, is joined to his wife and the two are united as one.*
>
> Ephesians 5:31 (NIV)

Money

I have read that couples contemplating marriage should have a map for a marital partner. I cannot say definitively whether this is right or not. I do say there must be an honest direction so that when a shift comes, the baseline can be revisited. There should not be thoughts of "I wish I had known." It would be fair to say my Aunt Remelle, who considered herself a matchmaker, did have a map. But her map was not ours. She, thrice married, had strong views about age, money, social graces, home and other things she made up as she talked. Her views were strong about money - separate accounts - always. We listened to her views and respected them without embracing them. We knew our values about money; we talked about them even before saying, "I do."

Money management for us was about our values rather than how much we had. My salary was stable and greater than what James, as a small business owner, earned. He owned properties. I did not. Soon after we married, he made his assets joint-owned. Our decisions had to be joint, requiring us to plan, talk and be open. We did not have secrets about money. I managed the household budget. Each of us had our personal money accounts. We decided when major purchases were to be made and completed them together.

When Edgar was ready for high school, James and I agreed on private school, a major financial decision. We determined when our first home, located atop his business, was no longer suitable, and we decided to buy a house. James did not care about driving "old" cars. I did. This always called for long conversations before a choice was made. My late husband did not like debt. I did not mind having debt as long as we could meet the commitment without strain. We worked to have a few months saved for expenses beyond what was due. We did agree unequivocally not to live beyond our income.

Sex and Romance

Much has been written about sex, date nights, and all things romantic. I believe these to be important. However, neither James nor I would have identified ourselves as romantic. By that, I mean there was no public display of emotions or major gift giving. All expressions of intimacy were private in our bedroom, a place of rest and enjoyment. James' gift giving was spontaneous, a single flower without an occasion or a chocolate bar at the end of my day. James rubbed my feet until I slipped into sleep after a long day at work. He gave me cards over the course of our marriage, not for special occasions, just a card anytime. My greatest gift to my husband was my love, care, and attention to and for his well-being. I am not a physical gift giver. We remembered birthdays and celebrated anniversaries, some in major affairs. We invited 200 guests to a church concert and dinner for our 25 years of marriage. We were ready to share with everyone that we liked being married.

Engaging mutually in social activities will enhance marriage and protect against attention that may be directed to others. Different interests can provide growth for both, and they need not be a source of tension. Anything that separates marital partners, in my view, is not wise. James did not like "double dates." He viewed spending time as a "double date" immature. Our weekday hours were consumed with work and balanced with child rearing and activities in their schools. We preferred to spend weekend hours with Edgar or Nancy, and Sundays were spent in church worship. We were homebodies, something we learned before marriage. We preferred time together alone - attentiveness, mindfulness, kindness, and genuine desire for the mutual comfort of each other. Our love and intimacy remained undisturbed for close to 50 years by putting each other before ourselves, saying 'Thank you' for pleasures, respecting each other, and being mindful of language. James was my greatest encourager. We did not joke or make demeaning or degrading comments to each other. Ours was a personal attentive life. As Mark Twain said, "To get the full value of joy, you must have someone to divide it with."

Child-Rearing and Grand Parenting

Children are a gift to a union. I don't believe there is another relationship with more opportunity than child-rearing for developing well-adjusted beings. Like marriage, rearing children is hard work and I say again, it is not for selfish or lazy people. Rearing children in marriage can be challenging and rewarding. I am not sure the balance is equal, however, I do believe the early formation of our children has its foundation in the home in which they are reared. Nothing is more formative for a child than the model they see early and participate in before they know much more about anything. Edgar and Nancy were reared in our marriage, but they were not a part of our relationship. Our children, born nine years apart with distinct personalities, required different nurturing. Rearing our children involved how we had been reared. Our personalities, which called us to talk quite a lot, sometimes every day about some aspects of child-rearing, sometimes caused tension. Thankfully, James and I did not fall back on the how of our personal rearing as much as guiding Edgar and Nancy to develop into who they could be, shaped by values of love, attention, safety, and discipline. Our children were reared with them being a priority, just as we made each other a priority.

Children must be disciplined because their hearts are likely to be filled with mischief. As parents, we have the responsibility to teach our children the right path; even as we acknowledge parenting is more than discipline. Fortunately, James and I were not weak-willed. Our concerns for the safety and well-being of Edgar and Nancy outstretched the popular opinions of others. We modeled our personalities, did not invite our children's opinions, conducted punishment as appropriate to the behavior and remained aware of childish manipulations. The strength of our relationship allowed us to rear reasonable, well-adjusted adults.

The Bible says, "Children are a gift from the Lord" (Psalm 127:3a). Our children were gifts to our marriage as we nurtured and grew with them and we ourselves became closer. We got this done with love for each other, Edgar, Nancy, Emerson, Abby, and Welton. Grandchildren are the crowning glory of the aged.

> *...bring your children up in the training and instructions of the Lord.*
>
> Ephesians 6:4b (NIV)

A Job as a Part of Marriage

I hear the term, "work husband" or "work wife" quite a lot. These terms are confusing to me. We only have one spouse, the person we marry. Sharing our days of work with our spouse eliminates a need to share deeper feelings with anyone else. I don't mean to say research initiatives are not shared or mutual issues should not be discussed with a colleague or that vetting and analyzing problems should not be done. Spousal conversations about workday situations strengthen the martial bond. As momma said, "Nothing is too good or too bad to tell your husband."

For most of our years of marriage, I worked in leadership or executive positions. James was my confidante and greatest encourager. I did not have a "work husband." I talked about everything that happened in my days with my husband. He did not know health care, the industry I served, but he knew me, my temperament, my stress levels and ethic. Talking with James stabilized my questioning thoughts, guided my relationships with men and helped me to navigate racism. No one alive was a greater partner in my work as much as my husband was. I considered our conversations about work an act of respect.

While we were not a part of the social circle of my workplace, James willingly joined me at events that were necessary. He knew whom I liked, whom I trusted, and whom I did not like or trust. He knew people in my workplace who injured my feelings and those who were "friends." Our daily conversations helped him to listen acutely to what a colleague might say about a situation or me. When we arrived at home, he offered his perspective, which almost always assisted in my decisions. I have not always been a good discerner about people, but James was. His inclusion as an observer of my workplace through a social lens enhanced our relationship.

Staying Power

The staying power of marriage is in an ability to adjust, adjust, and make more adjustments as two different, yet committed people live into mutual relationship. Marriage is a dance with alternating lead partners. Sometimes the dance is a waltz, sometimes a jitterbug, sometimes it's just holding and swaying with the music, and sometimes it even feels and looks as if the partners are dancing to a different beat.

Sometimes we step on a toe and say "I'm sorry" as we dance on. Nevertheless, we stay on the dance floor, closely aligned, sharing the same intimate spaces. When I have read that the lack of sex in marriage is one of the top three reasons for divorce, I ponder why two people get married to sleep together and then move into separate bedrooms. Personally, I believe when bedrooms are separated, the marriage is as well. James was ill for 17 years, snored, awakened frequently and sometimes called out, but we slept in the same bed until he died. The warmth of our bodies diminished the agony of his ordeal for both of us. Staying married means that the couple shares the good and the not so good.

Marriage is not for selfish people. When we agree to the covenant of marriage we are no longer our own. Every part of our selves is affected with every action. Marriage was the commitment to be the best person I could be, as James became the best he could be and as we grew, we were strengthened to be greater than either of us could be alone. We decided early - no divorce! Having decided that neither of us would give the other up taught us how to live together in reasonable harmony. When I look back, I am impressed with how easy it was to be and stay married.

I have heard from many friends about the battle of household management, with one or the other feeling unhappy about chores. Managing household chores does not become a problem when there is enough money to hire someone to help. When not, deciding to match chores with skills and desires can eliminate tension. Acknowledging those things we prefer not to do allows a discussion of choices with a balanced perspective; not perfect, yet manageable.

As a woman reared by a mother who believed "the wife cooks," I cooked all our meals. Both of us valued a clean space. We cleaned together. I did not think a man should iron clothes, and I preferred not to iron. We hired someone to iron the clothes. Perhaps one of the greatest money management successes for us was shopping together. Both of us enjoyed shopping although not for the same things. If we were shopping for a car in which I had minor interest, the trip became a time to have dinner out. Shopping for food was a matter of time and necessity. James did the driving so we intentionally shopped Thursdays after I finished work.

Disagreements, tension and strain in a marriage are unavoidable. Fights (not physical) are healthy, cleansing and afterward, it is wonderful to make up. We fought privately, sometimes all night, refusing to sleep until a resolution was reached, talking until we reached a spot where we could meet. Others were not invited into our fights, not friends, not children, not parents, not counsel, not pastors. We knew our difficulties better than anyone and chose not to have a mediator. Early in our relationship we thought we were settling our differences ourselves.

As we matured, we learned God was guiding us. We shared a deep faith and service to our church community. Infirmities of others taught us to look deeply at our own, to learn to change, and to love more. James was stubborn as was I. Yet, he was easy to be married to. I was not. When we disagreed, one of us had to give in. Angry behavior was not an option. James had an ability to stand up to me, a characteristic I significantly respected, and I grew couragous in other aspects of my life by his example. Marriage is not a game of who wins the debate, but rather a mutual agreement or understanding. Faith is the guiding principle. Acceptance is the joy.

Marriage is hard work. The commitment to put another before oneself can only be achieved through a deep love, not physical attraction, not money, not position, social status or perceived power. By love, I mean a definition articulated in the Bible in 1st Corinthians 13:4-8:

Love never gives up. Love cares more for others than for self.

Love doesn't want what it doesn't have. Love doesn't strut.

Doesn't have a swelled head. Doesn't force itself on others.

Isn't always "me first," Doesn't fly off the handle,

Doesn't keep score of the sins of others, Doesn't revel when others grovel,

Takes pleasure in the flowering of truth, Puts up with anything,

Trusts God always, Always looks for the best,

Never looks back, But keeps going to the end.

(The Message)

No one achieves this love every day; it is the pattern that matters to stay married. James and I recognized we were the only persons with whom we wanted to spend our lives, and because we did, there was no risk. Wanting to be married to James never changed for me. The commitment, expectations, and reality came as we lived together from our core being.

Trials in Marriage

When the commitment of "until death do we part," or whatever language this statement implies is made, nothing in the vow can be more serious or confining. These words came true for James and me during a 17-year journey, when Alzheimer's Disease showed up in the 33rd year of our relationship. I became my husband's full-time caregiver. My vow refused to allow me to place him in a nursing home. I knew if it had been me with the disease, James would have not let me be placed in a nursing home.

Our long life of talking became a blessing for us. Because of this practice, I knew his thoughts and desires even when he could no longer articulate them. There are many days after being a widow for close to 14 years, when James' voice is still within my spirit and sustains me.

> *Human beings, with all our faults and failings, can thank God for the institution of marriage - a holy union.*
>
> J. Stephen Lang

FIVE

Wisdom from Racism

The wind that blows can never kill the tree God plants; it blows east; it blows west; the tender leaves have little rest, but any wind that blows is best.

The tree God plants strikes deeper root, grows higher still, spreads wider boughs, for God's good-will meets all it wants.

Lillie E. Barr

Many people have asked the question, "How did a black woman from the segregated south, educated as a nurse, become, in 1979, the Chief Operating Officer of an Ivy League medical school hospital, the Hospital of the University of Pennsylvania (HUP)?" I could say, "Would have been impossible without faith," but that response would be far too simple, even misunderstood. This is my story about the power of a loving God doing "what He pleases" with an ordinary person, as He has done throughout biblical history. Ordinary people of strong or weak faith in God have been used to do what

He wills. Ours is to follow; I did. And like Barr's poem, God planted me and the journey at HUP was "any wind that blew was best."

Who I am in God? More than what I knew but a Divine Spirit guided me to face and overcome the evil oppression of racism in the walls of this storied institution, HUP. Some who may read this story will say, "I did not know this, or what was going on," and that would be true. Many people have offered opinions about what they thought, but those thoughts may not be consistent with my tenure in HUP. My late husband is the only person who has ever known the entire story. He traveled every step of my journey at HUP with me. He can be credited for keeping me faithful, walking with me, holding my hand, securing my heart and daily encouraging me. "Don't let them discourage you." Faith in a loving God deserves the ultimate praise. Looking back over 28 years at HUP, there is not a clear sign of why I was placed there to do the work. I have accepted my service as the will of God.

Many have thought, even said, that my experience at HUP "must have been awful," or, "I cannot imagine what that must have been like." Yes, dealing with racism at HUP was often painful and difficult. But I faced this journey with James and spiritually Divine directions. The startling thing to me is that I realize now that I was not as close to God as I grew to be. But, God kept me strong and gave me courage I did not know I had.

Racism is oppressive, evil, angry, hateful, ignorant and egotistical. These are demonic emotions and if they are engaged, will undermine spiritual well-being. I could not, did not, allow this to happen to my inner spirit. I regularly talked with God, seeking direction about a lifelong lesson I have learned over and over again, to put God first in my inner spirit. I am a gifted professional, however, those gifts too came from God. My human gifts and education were informed by Divine Spirit.

Let me place my story in context. In 1959, 58 years ago, I accepted a Head Nurse position in Neurology at HUP, a decision made by my maternal Aunt Remell. My spirited Aunt said, "HUP was the best place to work in Philadelphia." America was in a racial war. The evening news was dominated with daily occurrences of riots, property destruction, demonstrations, and expressions of anger across the United States brought on by the fight for the civil rights of black Americans. Civil rights leaders were horribly killed, some as they returned home at night. Murders were not limited to black people, but anyone, regardless of race or status, who dared step in to deal with the all-encompassing hate of racism.

In 1963 Medgar Evers, a field worker/leader in the NAACP, was massacred as he returned home one evening. In that same year, President John F. Kennedy was assassinated as he rode in a motorcade in Texas, and in 1968, the Rev. Dr. Martin Luther King, Jr. was murdered as he stood on a balcony in Tennessee. Many men and women who are less publicly acknowledged were also killed. Michael Schwerner, Andrew Goodman and James Cheney were ambushed and killed when they went to the south to register black people to vote. This was a dark time in America, unsafe to be a person of color. We were experiencing, once again, how we, as black people, were devalued simply because of the color of our skin.

When I arrived at HUP, I knew what living in environments of hate was and could be. None of which had poisoned, infected or contaminated my inner spirit. I grew up in an oppressive segregated environment in Jacksonville, Florida, in the early 1930s. I had been exposed to any and every indignity of humanity to black people by southern whites. Women in our community, including my mother, served in homes of white people, cooking meals, cleaning homes, doing laundry, giving care to the children, but they were not allowed to enter the homes through the front door. As a child I watched daily as white guards pushed, hit and verbally abused black men chained together as they repaired roads or cleaned up trash. These black men, who were serving prison terms, were publicly humiliated and called the "chain gang" as if the conditions of the prison were not punishment enough. Among these atrocities, my parents taught their children to value themselves.

In 1954, my senior year at college, our sacred place of worship, the Chapel at Tuskegee University, was torched and burned by the KKK. Crosses were burned at the entrance of our campus because our Dean of Students, Dr.

Charles G. Gomillion was prominent in fighting racism in Alabama. Those times were so fearful that we could be attacked by the KKK, Tuskegee's administration restricted students from traveling alone on campus after dark. I lived in Alabama, a short drive from Mississippi where Emmett Till was murdered by a gang of deranged white men, allegedly because of whistling at a white girl. In 1955, when Mrs. Rosa Parks refused to give up her bus seat to a white man, we at Tuskegee were influenced and extended participants, giving money in the launch of the Civil Rights Movement.

There was not a single hospital in or near Tuskegee that would accept the students from Tuskegee for clinical practice to give care to white patients. Dr. Lillian Holland Harvey, Dean of our school, refused to have us restricted to only being allowed to take care of the "colored." Dr. Harvey arranged for us to have clinical training in the New York hospital system. While I had limited understanding in 1952 of what all of this meant, I did know the actions of the leaders of these white-operated hospitals were demeaning and devaluing. The School of Nursing at Tuskegee is a pioneer in bestowing the bachelor degree to students, many of whom were intellectually gifted. Students graduating from the School of Nursing did not fail Alabama licensing to be registered, achieving the highest scores in the state. Our competence and creditably were not an issue, our skin color was.

In 1959, I arrived at HUP with a history of racial discord, rejections, attempted humiliations and painful experiences free of expectations or entitlement, accepting a position in an organization governed, led and celebrated by Caucasians. Culture shock took on new meaning. The medical staff had two black male physicians and one black female physician: Dr. James Robinson, a surgeon; and Dr. Edward Cooper, an internist; and Dr. Helen Dickens, an obstetrician who would later become the Dean of Students in the Medical School. The nursing leadership was 100% white. Five staff nurses of color worked in other areas of the hospital. The support staff was almost totally populated by people of color: aides, assistants, men and women who served food and those who kept the environment clean. A few black women were clerks on patient units with a minority in technical positions.

To say I was alone would be an understatement of several centuries, but being alone was a part of who I am. I experienced professional isolation in HUP, but not damage to my spirit. Shy and introverted, I don't enjoy large groups, don't have a need to be included or seen, and I don't seek or need praise. I, then and now, have been endowed with a spiritual confidence to live in places and environments alone, yet I've been able to rise above the conditions because of an inner guide. I was subjected daily to petty acts and pranks, spoken slurs, verbal harassments, stares, and dismissive comments made to and about my skin tone, my hair and other indignities I choose not to say. My deep faith sustained me and inner courage rooted my resolve. I kept close in my heart the words of Daddy, "you can do anything you want." God was present and not seeking me as a consultant. Mine was to trust and to be watchful.

> *Trust in the Lord with all your heart and lean not on your understanding. In all your ways acknowledge Him and He will make your paths straight.*
>
> Proverbs 3:5-6 NIV

Before HUP, I had only worked in hospitals that were owned and operated by black people. John Andrew Memorial Hospital served the college community of Tuskegee University. The now-closed Flint Goodridge Hospital served black people from a local community, and served as a training location for nursing students of Dillard University. Daddy and Momma taught us not to expect fair treatment or even humane behavior from Caucasians. I was not surprised by the lack of acceptance, nor upset or disappointed by the behavior of many in HUP who made it their job to devalue my experience and leadership. As ugly and demeaning as racism is, it was not hidden in the southern United States. The HUP environment was pretentious and patronizing. I had to make choices to not be labeled by the opinions of anyone, including those persons in the nursing administration. I engaged with people absent a need to explain myself or debate their ignorance.

I began work in HUP long before laws of workplace harassment were in place, thought of, or addressed. Superiority blinds most people to ignorance and in HUP there was no short supply of attitudes of being better than. Most nurses in leadership positions were graduates from the HUP School of Nursing with limited experience beyond those walls. Superior attitudes were a result of not knowing any better. I later discerned that insecurity and feeling threatened by an outsider among them added to their discomfort.

HUP did not have a single policy to address matters of racism in the workplace. After all, this was an Ivy league institution and anyone who worked in these walls should consider themselves to be privileged, whether they were black or white. I never experienced "privilege" to work at HUP. I was paid to do a job which I did well and never felt the need to give honor. I am shaped to value myself, anchored in this formation of being "fearfully and wonderfully made" (Psalms 139:14a NIV). My Dad's teaching in my formative years unpinned resilience, making it able to move above and beyond those who set out to demean my person.

> *It is not by chance or circumstance but by fitting our spirit to the circumstance in which God has placed in that we can be reconciled to life and duty.*
>
> F.W. Robertson (1816-1859)

Expectations can be a barrier. There is a saying, "Change your thoughts, change your life." I expected nothing from the HUP leadership other than equal and fair compensation. I expected of myself excellency in doing the job I accepted. I did not expect inclusion and do not remember a situation in which I felt excluded. Monumental Baptist Church was my spiritual anchor with my closest friends coming from that community. I chose not to compare my work with others or to seek praise. I came to HUP from leadership positions. I was pondering personal uncertainty about whether I should continue that path. I had no expectations on integrating HUP nursing leadership or being first or anything more, although history shows both were true. I had accepted a job; family formation, spiritual urgings and professional ethics said it had to be done. My expectations from and in HUP were limited so there were almost no disappointments. I did my job with inner empowerment, not external acclamation.

Aunt Remelle said, "HUP was the best place to work," and I accepted her word. She was a woman of courage, with a strong Christian faith, a registered nurse, a resident of Philadelphia most of her life, and greatly concerned for my future. She told me I had to be a "charge nurse." Her wisdom has been a life lesson. Leadership changes cultures. My Aunt reviewed my experiences and recognized that my innate ability to lead would be the only pathway for me in this hospital. She was my angel from God.

Julia Talmadge, then Director of Nursing at HUP, interviewed me. She and I walked through the halls of this massive complex as Julia proudly explained the "history, standards and achievements" of the nurses. She said, "You will be proud to work with them." Julia's tone expressed the "privilege" endemic at the time to work in this storied institution. Patients were organized in units by specialty: medical, surgical, obstetrical, intensive care, and pediatrics. HUP closed its pediatrics unit when the Children's Hospital moved from South Philadelphia and located next door to HUP several years later. As we walked the halls, Julia, a person of significant ego and persona told me, "You are over-qualified to be a staff nurse. I only have one job open, Head Nurse in Neurology."

We walked to the basement of a now demolished building to the Neurology Unit. The good lighting could not overcome the drabness of this unit. As we walked down a long corridor, I could see in the rooms, men and women who appeared very ill, and they were. Housed in two- and four-bed rooms in this dismal place were men and women who suffered from incurable diseases. When we left the Neurology Unit, Julia walked with me to the nurse's locker room telling me, "We will assign you a locker. We prefer you not wear a uniform in the street." This was orientation to nursing at HUP.

Every morning after listening to racial comments not directed to me but about me, I walked the short distance from the locker room to the Neurology Unit, passing broken equipment, stretchers, sometimes trash, and lockers no longer in use. I entered the Neurology Unit to be greeted by a nurse who could hardly wait to leave. No one "wanted to work in Neurology," Julia had told me. As the only professional nurse for 28 patients, I depended upon the assistants and aide, most of whom had been at HUP for many years, all my senior by age. I planned with this support staff service for these men and women in our care, some of whom were either too sad or barely able to speak because of diseases such as, Myasthenia Gravis, Multiple Sclerosis, Guillan Barre', post-stroke syndrome, or Lou Gehrig' s disease.

I grew possessive of these men and women, giving them the best professional and compassionate service I could. I got to know their families and the pain they were experiencing. These men and women, the nurse assistants and I, in combined balance and value, faced the challenges inherent in these diseases. There are some things we never forget. One of our patients, a woman who worked as a bank teller in her mid-50s with Lou Gehrig's disease, said to us one afternoon, "I will die, but I am thankful to be here with you." Racism did not rob us of this opportunity to give this white lady our best.

No one can have a true idea of right until he does it.

James Martineau

Many days I did not eat lunch, not because I was not hungry but because I was the only professional nurse on the unit. The scheduler in the nursing office "forgot" to send a nurse. Leaving the unit would have compromised the safety of patients. I never got an apology just her "I forgot." I refused to call Ruth Marshall and ask for lunch relief, instead, when I did eat, I ate lunch in the corner of the nurse's station out of sight of others. I am not a big eater. Except that I knew I needed to eat, this slight did not have significant harm.

I could not compromise my dignity, formation, or spiritual principles to accommodate the behavior of others. Discipline gave me tremendous strength doing what I agreed to do and doing it well, respectfully and by Divine order. I never considered that I was doing anything unique. I lived out who I am, even as I recognized every hateful act. I don't recall being angry, maybe disgusted or amused, but not angry. Faith in God kept me centered.

> *All the water in the ocean cannot sink a ship unless it gets inside.*
>
> Eugene Peterson

I read the life of Oswald Chambers many times, not just his devotionals, but his life story. Even as Chambers died at a young age, his writings have served many as a mentor, including me. I cared for, supported, and yes, loved these men and women in Neurology who seemed to have little hope. I lived Chambers title, "My Utmost for His Highest." I don't deny racism, ugly as it was and can be. I refused to let others define me, give titles they chose, or attach themselves to "a black friend."

> *For I know the plans I have for you, declares the Lord, plans to prosper you and not harm you.*
>
> Jeremiah 29:11 (NIV)

The Divine Being indeed knew the plans. Among those people who were mean spirited, I also had advocates who dimmed the ugliness. The doctors appreciated the care given to their patients and advocated to have my service broadened. Without any reason I could see, I got promoted after 18 months at HUP. I moved from Neurology with 28 patients to Tenth Gates, an all private room unit where 42 people of "means" were housed. I continue to lead, teach and give care to the men and women who entrusted themselves to us. I did not care how much money it was said they had. I did care about our quality of care. Three years later I was promoted to supervise the "medical units" Julia described in my interview, 225 patients housed in 7 medical units.

Professionalism, honest relationships, superb care and ease in working with me motivated several doctors to recommend that I be promoted. Relationships matter, especially when there is shared common purpose for others, not just personal advancement. In doing what I do best, I developed relationships across races, educational backgrounds and faith traditions, and gained tremendous respect.

Sometime in late 1974, I became restless in my work. One rainy Saturday morning I called Dorothy Clark, a nurse at Penn who had become a friend. I asked Dottie to pray for me to find something else to do, maybe I said "more responsibility, overseeing the support functions." She said, "I will." I wanted to get out of the nursing office, but not away from patients. Looking back, I know God heard those prayers. Chambers says, "God does not tell you what He will do, He reveals Himself to you."

In the spring of 1975, I received a call from the office of the Vice President of Health Affairs inviting me to a meeting later in that same day. The late Dr. Thomas Langfitt, the Vice President, had convened a group of people to begin work to divest the Graduate Hospital from HUP. At the time both were losing money, facilities were in disrepair and they were losing "market position." The late Mark S. Levitan had been appointed the leader of both hospitals. Mark had engaged consultants, attorneys, and financial experts to build his team. I was asked to join this team, but I had no idea why. I was told, "We need your history, and you tell it like it is." Years later Mark told me, "Dr. Arnold Relman, the Chairman of the Department of Medicine, recommended you."

I grew in wisdom as I navigated racism in HUP. Critical to my ability to not become angry or to allow being black to become a barrier for me or an asset for Penn, I had to be me to limit compromise to accommodate others, to be seated in my personal assets and to work for the good of others. Living out this wisdom led to being named the Director of Strategy and Planning for both Graduate Hospital and HUP, then five years later, the Chief Operating Officer. Along the way, the medical school leadership, the Dean, Dr. Edward Stemmler, the Chairs of the Clinical Departments in the School of Medicine, accepted me for the person I am. I was told long after I left HUP by a doctor, "We never knew how you kept personally balanced, pleasant and excellent." While I did not respond to this comment, I knew it was by Divine Spirit.

I know one person can make a difference, but that opportunity does not mean forever. There is a time to leave positions. Leaving is less problematic when there has not been an attitude of personal ownership of a position, whether you are black like me, or Caucasian, Hispanic, Asian or any other race or nationality. Institutions hire people to do work. Both accepting a position and leaving is a personal decision. For me, I did excellent work in each of the positions I held: Head Nurse, Strategist, and Chief Operating Officer.

Owning an institutional position is a trap for pain. Someone once told me, "Institutions have no loyalty." True, but we are to value ourselves, the work we do, and not expect acclaim. The work must speak for itself.

Racism is intact in American society. Demonic acts will continue in institutions, in education systems, the church, in housing, in lending practices, and I suspect every aspect of our society. We need not ignore its devastating behavior when we live into who we are. Writing this chapter, I reflected on the life of Jesus Christ as recorded in the Gospels of the New Testament in the Bible. People, who did not believe or agree with how and what Jesus did, killed Him. He did not compromise who He was, or is, or what He came to do. While I was never threatened with death, I chose to follow to a great extent the model of Christ as I navigated racism in HUP.

Faith underpinned and guided me through and beyond racism at HUP. One very cold morning I was walking east in Center City Philadelphia on Chestnut Street. I can no longer remember why. I heard a familiar voice call my name, "Delores, Delores." It was Julia Talmadge, a bit disheveled, and she was standing in a recessed area of the now demolished McCory Store at Juniper and Chestnut Streets. I stopped and asked, "How are you, Julia?"

She said, "Alright, just trying to get to the Reading Terminal for coffee." I said, "I'll walk with you." We walked down 13th Street to Market, crossed the street and entered the Reading Terminal Market at 12th and Filbert Streets. I treated Julia to breakfast.

As we sat, she eating her breakfast and I drinking coffee, Julia said, "I am so sorry."

Not sure what Julia was apologizing for, I responded, "About what?"

Julia said, "When I hired you, I was sure you would fail. I was wrong. I am so sorry."

I did not see Julia again before she died. At the time we shared this meal, I had retired from HUP and opened a business. The passage of time between her telling me, "You are overqualified," and then giving me a job she assumed I would fail at to this day, sitting with a fragile, disheveled woman, allowed me to receive and accept this revelation—What Julia meant for harm; God used for good.

Wisdom teaches me to be myself, the person God made me: black and female.

I am now 86 years old, and once again looking at hate across America. Even so, I resolve to be me. I suspect the evil of racism will always be with humanity until the world is no more. At the heart of unity is respect for every person God has made. I chose to respect me and all those around me in HUP for 28 plus years and also in the communities I now serve, not by title, position, or place in an organization. While I was often not respected in the early years at HUP, I respected everyone. I did not like everyone, I did not care to be friends with many, but respect for their person never wavered.

> *Be with God in outward work, refer them to Him, offer them to Him, seek to do them in Him and for Him and He will be with you in them. You will not be hindered, invite His presence into your soul. Seek to see God in all things. He will keep you, reveal to you things He could not show you until now.*
>
> E.B. Pusey

In 2013, I was asked to be a participant on a "Search" Committee for an Executive Presbyter in Philadelphia. I accepted with significant reluctances. The gift of accepting was the opportunity to work with the Reverend John Willingham, Pastor of the Doylestown Presbyterian Church. John and I became friends. He introduced me to his wife, Lori, and we too became friends.

One Sunday, I decided to worship with them, and received in John's sermon a gift that further helped me make sense of my experiences at HUP. I asked John if I could use excerpts from this sermon, "Forgetful and Fruitful." With generous spirit he responded, "Of course," and Lori sent his sermon. Because the sermon is so akin to my HUP experience, I close this chapter on Racism with significant gratitude for John's text. Wisdom guides forgetful and gives fruitful.

A Word…
"Forgetful and Fruitful" *Genesis 41:46-57*

Over the course of our summer worship, we are following the Old Testament story of Joseph. We began by reading about troubles of his own making when he was a teenager and last Sunday heard of the moment thirteen years later when he began the role for which God had been preparing him all that time. Those verses told of how Pharaoh, King of Egypt, had experienced two troubling dreams and only in retrieving Joseph from prison did he gain insight into what the nocturnal messages meant. The falsely-incarcerated man not only provided an interpretation – 7 years of abundant harvests followed by 7 years of famine – but also a plan for the hard times. The king was so impressed that he immediately selected Joseph to oversee the effort, named him second in command only to himself, arranged a marriage with the daughter of a priest, and then installed the Hebrew man to that position of prominence and responsibility.

Our passage resumes the narrative at that point as the author covers fourteen years in only twelve verses. The time of abundant harvests come just as Joseph has said and grain is stored in cities across the land. Thus, when the famine years arrive as predicted, the people of Egypt still have bread as Joseph opens the storehouses and sells grain to locals and others in the region too. The plan has worked and Pharaoh's trust in Joseph has been vindicated.

The telling of those events is likely the primary intent of this narrative, offering not only the biblical explanation for why Joseph was brought to Egypt, but also setting the stage for the great reunion with his siblings which will soon occur. Yet in the middle of describing a well-executed government program, we are given a glimpse into Joseph's personal life too, as during the years of abundance, his wife and he welcomed two sons. He calls them Manasseh and Ephraim explaining the first name to mean, "God has made me forget all my hardship and all my father's house," and the second, "God has made me fruitful in the land of my misfortunes."

With those names, Joseph makes two profound statements, as there had been much hardship for him – being sold by his brothers and sold again to Potiphar, of being placed into prison on trumped-up charges and forgotten there for two years. Thus, his first-born carried a name that celebrated how God had allowed Joseph to forget all that heartache. The name of his second son proclaimed that there has been profound success for Joseph too, both vocationally and personally as he has risen from slavery to a position of great authority and fatherhood, acknowledging God as the author of that outcome too. In both names, Joseph gave thanks for the activity of his Maker – lifting up both what he could now forget and what he could not celebrate – pointing himself back to God.

In our best moments, we do the same thing. In our most faithful times, we are able to forget the hurts that have come our way, and those who have brought them upon us. That isn't an easy thing to do as instead of forgetting such hardships, sometimes we might be prone to replay the wrongs, the missed changes or hurtful words spoken by others.

In our best moments too, we are able to point to God as the source of all our abundance celebrating the way God has provided us with talents and friends, loved ones and most of all, eternal life in Christ. Still, one can also overlook or ignore God's part in our successes, believing instead that all of our accomplishments arise solely from our hard work and commitment.

I suspect both challenges were present in Joseph too, so in those names he offered both a testimonial and a reminder that what had come about was due to the powerful work of God. Joseph was declaring that, on his own, he could not have forgotten about the troubling events of his past and instead could have used his new position of authority to exact revenge. On his own, Joseph might have believed that the only reason he was now so powerful was due to his smarts and skill owing no gratitude to God or anyone else. In giving those names to Manasseh and Ephraim, however, that former slave proclaimed he could be forgetful and fruitful only because of God. Witnessing every time he spoke their names to how God had accomplished what Joseph could not have done on his own. Our lives reveal the same truth.

Some of you will recall a true story that our friend Don Howland told in a sermon here during the year he served as our pastoral assistant. The story is not his as he faithfully attributed it to Craig Dykstra, a Presbyterian minister who serves on the faculty of Duke Divinity School. The account itself, though, recalls a moment from his time as a student at Princeton Seminary.

"I was living with this wonderful elderly woman of considerable means," Dykstra recalls, "who rented rooms in her spacious home to impoverished graduate students the likes of me. In her dining room, standing alone in a reserved space on the buffet under the gleam of recessed accent lights, stood a crystal vase of Steuben glass...She loved the vase and so did I. Steuben glass and I had not been entirely strangers," he pointed out. "Even before I moved into her home, I used to take the train from Princeton to Manhattan every now and again, and I'd walk down Fifth Avenue with its great stores…the Steuben Glass store was there too, and more than once I'd wander in to gaze in its darkened rooms, more museum than store. I would gasp at the price tags: one thousand dollars for this vase, five thousand for that one, ten thousand for the little crystal polar bears. I'd been exposed to Steuben before although since we traveled in different social circles [this woman's home] was the first time we were living together up close and personal.

"You know what I'm going to say next," Dykstra went on, "But it wasn't my fault. There was another graduate student living in that home at the time, and one day, when our landlady was out of town for a week and the other student was washing out the remains of some tulips from the Steuben, she dinged it on the sink. A one-inch triangle of glass broke from its rim, and the rest of it cracked from the center point of the triangle all the way down to its base. The other graduate student, even more economically destitute than I, could only cry. We left it in all its pathos on the kitchen counter, sick to death at what had happened.

"Our landlady returned," he says "found her beloved vase where we'd left it, and found herself understandably enough, a little broken as well. She wasn't angry so much as bereaved and for days which turned to weeks, she left it lying there in state on the kitchen counter, unable to bring herself to do the inevitable. 'Maybe they can fix it somehow,' she would say from time to time, looking for any glimmer of encouragement from me. 'You can't repair broken crystal,' I'd reply, realistic to the core. And she knew it too…

"I think I'm going to call up Steuben to see if they might not be able to fix it,' she said to me one more time. I tried to keep from rolling my eyes," Dykstra recalled. "Undaunted by my response, call up Steuben she finally did. She told them, 'I love the vase and I know it's crazy and all, but wondered if you might have some suggestion as to what I might do.' 'We're sorry for your loss,' Steuben said,' but the vase you're describing is no longer in production.' What Steuben did next took our breath away. What they said was this: 'If you'll bring the broken vase up to our store, our artists can fashion a replacement at our expense. We will copy and replace it at no charge.' Steuben," Dykstra concluded in amazement, "would bear the high cost of what we ourselves had broken." (Dykstra, Craig. "The Unreality of God," 10/31/99)

That's what we celebrate this day too, not a repaired vase, but the one who brought about healing and joy for Joseph long ago and has done the same for us. Which is why our best response is simply to stop and offer our praise once more to the one who has given us life in Christ, celebrating all the ways God has done what we could never have done for ourselves.

Reverend John Willingham, Pastor
Doylestown Presbyterian Church

~ SIX ~

Wisdom of Leadership

One evening, Barbara Warrington, H. Ray Welch and I were having dinner at the Butcher and Singer Restaurant in Philadelphia, Pennsylvania, to celebrate Barbara's appointment to a new position. Ray and I had jointly coached Barbara during a transition in her career. At the time of Barbara's decision to transition, the three of us served the same institution: Barbara was a Vice President in the corporate office, Ray, President of a system of five hospitals, and I served as a member of the Board of Trustees of the hospital system. Ray and I, over the course of several months, helped Barbara to match her skill set with a position better suited than the one she occupied. She accepted our coaching and in time became a Chief Executive Officer in a New York City not-for-profit organization. During the first course of our dinner, Barbara asked, "What has made your leadership successful?"

Without a delay, Ray responded, "By being myself." His simple sentence defined a central element of effective organizational leadership by expressing a personal characteristic critical to determining how we effectively lead.

As I reflected on this chapter, my attention turned to leaders like Ray and others with whom I have been privileged to be associated for over 60 years of my career. Over this span of years, I grew to define leadership that may or may not meet a textbook definition. I define effective leaders as those women and men who use personal skills and gifts, and model the value of human relationships to meet the mission of an institution. These women and men integrate their inner being with an outer world. They have vision with broad perspectives about what they undertake to do, and they accept the requirement for emotional and spiritual preparation for leading. While educational preparation is essential, it does not replace experience, integrity, personal concern for other humans, or wisdom. I worked with a magnificent leader, Mark S. Levitan, who often said, "Leadership needs gray hair," a statement for maturity.

It is not coincidental that high performing organizations, when looking for a new leader, will seek demonstrable experience. Most humans overrate themselves when seeking a leadership position. The responsibility to examine those opinions is the first responsibility of owners of the institutions, the not-for-profit or corporate board. The library is well resourced with books on leadership, many of which I have read myself. As valuable as they are, none makes leaders. Maybe they produce scholars on leadership, but not leaders who can lead. Selected leaders because of family connections, social status, name recognition, friendships, or sometimes, former titles, does not guarantee they can lead. I recently spent time with a woman who had reasonable success in one area, and who, because of a lack of self-awareness, believed she could be president of a college. When not offered the position, she was greatly disappointed.

Failure in leadership is an opportunity for growth if we willingly open ourselves to our inner work. We seek opportunities to learn that which we do not know, to engage an advisor, or to study books that teach us how to enhance our knowledge. Leadership capacity is strengthened when we listen. Sometimes, those who are not supposed to know can enhance our work if we listen. Listening to the voices of others gives me a good indication of how they feel about a situation. It also reminds me to look within to discover how I feel, rather than assuming their feelings are the truth.

During my career as a consultant, I worked with a leader who expanded his authority with abandon because of an overvalued opinion of self. In his zeal to outpace other hospital leaders in the Philadelphia marketplace, he assumed authority beyond a defined scope and engaged in practices that resulted in the closing of one hospital and a storied medical school for women. In the aftermath of his leadership, it became clear that funds restricted for other purposes were violated, limiting opportunities to only those that could be met with the funds that remained. His zeal to be a leader outpaced his knowledge of the Philadelphia health care market.

Effective leaders know how to delegate authority consistent with responsibility and empower others to do what they have been asked to do. People who have an understanding of the scope of authority rarely go in wrong directions. Those who do not create chaos.

Grumblings are limited when expectations are clear for oneself and for those who serve. I met expectations based on personal values of clarity and integrity. Compromise was not accepted, rather I found a way of waiting quietly until change could be made. Expecting to be liked as a leader is a mistake. Leadership behavior is doing what is right, just, and fair. Leadership, Mark Levitan often said, "is not a place to win star status." Leading toward the delivery of the mission is the right thing.

Effective leaders must know who they are, the inner core of self, the self they are when no one is looking. As important as educational qualifications must be, equally as important is understanding personal biases. This demonstrates integrity, and shows you have confidence, inner security and values. Knowing what we do not know guides effective leaders to select people to work with who are more knowledgeable. Control in any form disrespects another person. Effective leaders do not control, rather they guide, teach, model and hold others accountable all while expressing respectful concern for other persons. Emotionally insecure persons in leadership positions decrease productivity, damage morale, and can unintentionally close institutions. Leadership matters and requires emotional security and maturity.

Someone recently asked me, "Is a leader made or born?" I do not know the answer to that question. I do know we behave out of who we are, and furthermore, character and integrity are critical to how we apply knowledge.

Challenges That May Face Women

As a woman in a world led by men, noise from my external environment was a daily distraction for me. Appointed Chief Operating Officer (COO) at the elite, storied Hospital of the University of Pennsylvania (HUP), I had to be a leader. Not a black leader, not a nurse, not a woman, not a token, not a person to be toyed with, rather a competent person whose responsibility was to ensure excellent care to those who entered our doors. The most important gift for me to lead HUP was, as Ray said, "being myself." At that time in the history of HUP, my leading the operational management made history for the University of Pennsylvania. No other hospital across America had the distinction of a woman operating as leader with the authority vested in the COO except those sponsored by religious communities. I did not have a female peer, mentor, model or advisor. I did have James, my husband, who supported and encouraged me on my way. Perhaps it is because of James that I did not fear losing a job or not being accepted, and I could be me.

Effective leaders know they need authentic advisors, people who know as much as they know or more, who are not seeking attention for themselves and have appropriate loyalty in relationship. Many leaders select "staff" from a friendship network. While I don't judge those decisions, that selection was not for me. I preferred men and women with competencies for the work to be done and with respect for my leadership. I found it critically important to be surrounded by men and women who knew themselves, did not "kiss up," and held people we served as highest priority. Experience led me to select men and women I could trust. Sometimes I failed in judging this critical characteristic and had to fire someone, and I did so without hesitation.

I inherited an associate who was more knowledgeable in finance than I was. He had expected to be appointed to the position of COO. When this did not happen, he set out to report to the Chief Executive how operations management could be improved. This associate chose to ignore my leadership even as he was overly complimentary. When I learned of these attempts, I fired him. Effective leaders select, guide and promote men and women who express and live out competencies. Complimenting the boss is a behavior some men seem to engage in with women leaders. This is not a competency.

I only had to fire one man because of his attempt at flattery. I had a colleague known among some as a womanizer. One morning as we entered a conference room for a strategy meeting he said, "I will not be able to pay attention this morning, Delores. You look too good. I love red." This colleague actually believed he was right to tell me he could "not concentrate" because of the way I looked. Since I had no intentions of trying to change my looks and he had not been hired to help me choose clothing, but as a construction manager, my option was to give him the opportunity to use his skills with another institution that was not HUP. I fired him for inappropriate behavior.

Others who wanted to be employed at HUP no longer took a risk of inappropriate compliments. Listening to the voices of others informs how others may feel and is a good indication to look at self-awareness. As a woman leader in a male world populated by some who chose to play to femininity, it was important for me to set standards and not accept such behavior. Knowing who I am reduced this challenge and I became a colleague, not one who could be patted on the head, expected at "happy hour," or who would attend dinners that were not business focused.

As COO, I had responsibility to oversee the renovation of aged buildings and the construction of new ones. I could not read a blueprint and was aware I needed help. I was privileged to have the late Ralph Murphy help me to learn and enhance my work. One afternoon Ralph and I attended a planning meeting for new construction. As we left the meeting Ralph said, "My boss must be sure about blueprints. They will lead to design and eventually cost." With blueprints stretched before us, he pointed to the south, north and west of the drawings as he admonished me saying, "Lose fear, this is not rocket science."

Listening to and being guided by Ralph was a gift that served the next ten years of planning facilities at HUP – the Silverstein Pavilion, Founders Building, renovations to Ravdin, Dulles, and Maloney buildings. Ralph taught me how to rearrange the traffic patterns of the main first floor of the HUP extensive building landscape.

When I was appointed to lead operations at HUP, the late Mark Levitan, Chief Executive Officer asked me, "Delores, what do I need to do to help you succeed?" I said, "Empowerment. Signature authority for payroll checks, control of the budget, presence at all meetings where decisions are likely for the operations, and the authority for policy development and execution for everyone who works here." Knowing myself and having learned from a failed earlier experience in New Orleans taught me to understand the need for appropriate authority to be effective. As a minority nurse in this Ivy League institution, race and gender were called out hourly. Controlling these aspects of HUP was required. Had Mark said no, I would not have made history. Personal (inner) security, maturity, and knowing myself served my success as much as my competencies.

Relationship and Leading

Mixing friendships and professional life can be a formula for disaster. I have experienced with others compromised decisions in such instances, pain and damage with broken relationships. For myself, I was fortunate to lead my children in my business for close to 15 years. Nancy and Edgar served as associates, and along the way, I guided and taught them what mission-focused work is to be. In the years after I closed the business, Edgar became a Human Resources leader, then a church administrator, and later a business owner which serves seniors in transition. I am his listener as he continues to lead and thrives.

Nancy worked closely with our business with a loose title of administrator. She did everything to make me a successful business woman. She led without knowing she did. A primary doctor, Nancy now is Chief Medical Officer of Mazzoni Health Center in Philadelphia. Perhaps the greatest testament to my leadership is an invitation to coach my daughter when she decided to be a medical leader. We were recently discussing a leadership issue. As I listened to her articulation of an issue, I was overjoyed.

My children and I became closer friends as they became effective leaders without damaging our genetic relationships. I was indeed fortunate because both my children brought to their jobs maturity and competence.

However, in many cases, I would caution people against hiring family members. Sometimes such hirings can do irreparable damage to the relationship and sometimes they compromise the institution. And sometimes both. At a minimum, they produce awkwardness between the other staff members and the relatives.

Encouragement to be who you are as a leader is my wisdom gift to aspiring leaders, seasoned leaders, and those who have led.

Hard work means prosperity.

Proverb 13:4a

SEVEN

Wisdom of Aging

Gray hair is a crown of glory; it is gained by living a godly life.

Proverbs 6:31

Della and I were sipping tea and eating a cookie as we sat, talking about aging. We were expressing to each other our hopes for a "good" aging when Della said, "I don't want to spend my time with doctors."

At the time of our conversation, Della was in the 9th decade of her life and I in the eighth of mine. Both of us have lived active lives, making choices that matched our inner spirit. Della, in this simple sentence, expressed a desire to continue a personal focus, setting the stage for this period of our lives. We have gained wisdom, we recognize matters which are most important, and, (not to be morbid, but realistic, simple and independent), we realize that time is limited. Every time I read the Proverbs verse cited, I remember our conversation and Della's beautiful gray hair, and that we were both beyond the time promised in Scripture.

> *The length of our days is seventy years or eighty if we have strength.*
>
> Psalms 90:10-NIV

The Bible, in my reading, does not talk about retirement. It does say quite a lot about aging. Beginning in Genesis Chapter 5, it records the lives/genealogy from Adam to Noah. Everyone is old, yet some continue to produce children, and Noah, being obedient to God, constructed an Ark that changed humanity. Adam, the first man to be created by God, had a child at 130 years old. Enoch was born when his father was 162 years old. Methuselah lived until he was 960 years old having fathered Lamich when he was 187 years old, and other sons and daughters at 782 years old. Lamich fathered Noah at 182 years old.

Noah at 500 years old (Genesis 5:22) fathered sons. When God wanted a special job done—building the Ark—he called Noah (Genesis 6:9-22). These old men, remaining active in their old age, inspire me. I have been inspired by the life of Moses since childhood, especially the "burning bush" story and God's speaking with him. Now in the eighth decade of life, my biblical mentor is Moses, who at 80 years old was called to lead the Israelites out of Egypt. Moses' story begins in Exodus Chapter 2 expanding through Leviticus, Numbers and Deuteronomy. He died when he was 120 years old (Deuteronomy 34:7 NIV).

While reading about these men, I have been inspired that we can "bear fruit in old age," which doesn't mean birthing children, rather making contributions for and to the good of others. The story of Moses determined a decision for me, when, at the age of 80, I accepted an assignment to assist historic black theological schools. This assignment has blessed my life, given me new friends and engaged my time and gifts in matters of my heart, God and the Church. I have traveled many miles doing this service relatively free of any problems. Aging does not mean we are to stop. God decides when we stop. Aging does mean accepting bodily changes, mental fatigue, freeing oneself from undue stresses and following the commands of God.

They will bear fruit in old age; they will stay fresh and green.

Psalm 92:14 (NIV)

American society does not value aging as much as some others. We encourage retirement, and even "buy out" those who are seasoned in some organizations. Wisdom is not valued, economics is. Beauty is associated with youth and while that may be true, a beautiful spirit far outweighs physical attributes. I acknowledge I am not, nor have I ever been, a fan of excessive make-up, colored hair or variations of hair God did not give me, or changes made by plastic surgery. I have an acquaintance who told me she had "plans to sue Medicare." When I asked why, she said, "They will not cover the cost of having my eyelids lifted." Medicare refused to pay because this woman was 80 years old, and the eye surgery was cosmetic. I enjoy exercise for good health, but not as an attempt to make my body over. I dress well, get my hair done every week, and my nails manicured every other week. Wisdom has informed me not to attempt to correct what I have been given by God, rather to celebrate and live into the gift of life. We can do all sorts of things to ignore aging, but the fact is, although you may change your appearance, you cannot change your age.

Literature on how to age well is all around us. Most of the studies are authentic, surveying people, quantifying data and coming to conclusions most of which can benefit us in managing our minds and bodies. Social engagement and relationships are, in most lists, strongly encouraged as things to do as we age. I agree with this recommendation. I have many conversations with men and women who, after retirement, could not find satisfaction in volunteer work and provided social engagement, and if volunteering could not be aligned with one's gifts or an unmet desire, find their satisfaction limited. On the other hand, those who view volunteering as a service to others report finding joy.

Aging with grace calls for a daily celebration of the bodies we have and calls us to be deliberate in how we live in our bodies, recognizing that our bodies house the soul. Our body and mind are not separable – a healthy mind is a healthy body. Many people say age is a number;

I say these persons have never been old. Aging is more than a number, rather aging is the chance to face our senior years and determine our life's quality, to stay "fresh and green." We age well by being deliberate in how we manage relationships, our health, and the use of our time. I have found it necessary to limit relationships and even conversations which drain energy, deciding instead to talk with those who are refreshing. I make room for time with persons of common purpose. I end relationships when someone tells me more than two times that I should "get rest" or do something they think is good for me even as that person may be less healthy than I am. Independence is important to me. American society encourages creating dependency of aged persons, and not wellness. While we must be reasonable, I will not allow other's views to deter me. Uninformed opinions waste precious time and establish attachments that don't add to the quality to life.

Aging sometimes brings stiffness anywhere from my spine to my extremities. My body aches if I sit for long periods. I place my phones and a glass of water some distance from my chair, which requires me to stand and move to answer the phone or to get a drink of water, eight glasses a day. Exercise gives many benefits to our aged bodies. We can design a plan that best helps our bodies and suits our spirits.

In good weather, I walk to errands, and when unable to walk outside I do so inside. Walking clears my head and increases oxygen in my blood, thus enhancing my concentration and my thinking. Yoga is great for balance, is strengthening, and can be fun. I take yoga classes twice a week. I add to planned exercise by doing my own house cleaning, opting to use a service monthly for deep cleaning. Carrying grocery bags can add strength to upper body. I shop a couple times a week and carry moderately weighty bags a block from the market, taking deep breaths as I put food away.

Some of us lose height as we age, or our feet may sometime press. My feet do drag, and I have lost two inches of height. Changes such as these require adjustments if we are to keep ourselves "fresh and green." The cabinets in my home have all been rearranged to eliminate stepladders. I love oriental rugs and would miss them if required to give them up. To keep myself safe and maintain my rugs, they are secured to the floor to decrease a possibility of a fall.

Healthy weight is critical to good health. Being overweight can damage our knees, lead to hypertension, diabetes, and other health problems. Controlling weight is a matter of management and behavior. Cooking healthy meals when eating at home and carefully selecting what is ordered when eating out is key to weight control. My friend, Dr. Susan Leath, told me a long time ago, "most weight problems are due to fork lifting." She is correct. We gain weight because we eat too much or make unhealthy choices. I love cake, but limit how often I eat a slice. I watch portion size rather than limit what I enjoy. It is a rare Saturday when I don't eat a piece of fried chicken or enjoy a hamburger on the first Friday of many months when having lunch with my friend Paula Gross. I ate ice cream most of my life every night. Now at 86, I eat ice cream a few evenings a week and when dining out. I have accepted that eating too much ice cream is not my friend.

Managing our health is important no matter the age; true prevention is better than having to seek a cure. Effective health management requires a primary care doctor who partners with us to keep a balanced health status. Fortunately for me, I don't have many health challenges. Those that I do have are capably managed by Dr. Aba Barden-Maja, a friend for more than two decades. Dr. Barden is an ideal doctor for me, a perfect match for my independent spirit as she listens, but retains making the medical decisions. When I visit with her a couple times a year, I leave with clarity about what I am to do.

Social engagement is critical to aging gracefully and to mental well-being that comes from good relationships. Staying in touch with those you love and those who love you strengthens relationships as we engage socially. This does not cost anything or require work. I talk with my daughter Nancy every day and my son Edgar several times during a week. I talk with my non-genetic children, Lynette, several times a day and Bret, at least once a week, and Mary anytime. Emerson and Abby, my granddaughters, can be depended on for frequent chats during a month. I receive several visitors a week in my home, men and women who call me mentor. I engage in long chatty conversation some evenings with friends, and others across a day. I read the Bible, as well as books written by men and women who focus on matters of the spirit. I find kinship, mentoring and friends as I read.

Community is important to offset loneliness. Age has given us wisdom that, when used as a gift, enriches the lives of others. The evidence can be seen in the growth of communities for people past 50 years old and an increase in services for us as well. I engage in communities through worship in church, Bible classes, and lunch and conversation with friends and colleagues. Most Sundays I worship at First Presbyterian Church in Philadelphia where I serve as an Elder. When not at my church I worship with Nancy and her family at the St. Luke Episcopal Church. On occasion, I am invited by friends to worship at their church. I teach Bible classes once a week to residents who live in an apartment for senior citizens, often joined by members of my church and others. Once a month, ten women gather in my home for Bible study, prayer, brunch and fellowship.

These are just examples of what I do. I mention them to encourage you as you age to keep as many of your regular social interactions going as you can and add new ones if possible. You will sometimes want to make excuses for not going (I'm too tired or I'm too achy), but social engagements are an important part of healthy aging. So, get up, get dressed, and get going. You'll be thankful you did.

Sleep is important to the brain for it to rest, no matter our age. Our bodies need adequate sleep for effective functioning when awake. Planning regular bedtime is easy and controllable. I go to bed at 10 p.m. and get up between 6 and 7a.m. I don't receive telephone calls after 9:30, unless there is an emergency. Eight or more hours of sleep makes me effective, focused and responsive across the daytime. In my earlier work life, it was common for me to engage in activities for which I held myself accountable 10-12 hours a day. I now restrict activity to 6 hours a day, an adjustment to age and self-care accountability.

Everyone has their own inner clock telling them how much sleep they need. Figure yours out and then love your mind and body by giving them the restoration that sleep provides.

> *The glory of the young is their strength; the gray hair of experience is the splendor of the old.*
>
> Proverb 20:29

I am now 86 years old. Wisdom works. I become more and more aware of this the older I get. Perhaps the most important wisdom is knowing who I am and to whom I belong. Or, for you, my reader, for you to know who you are and to whom you belong. The inner spirit of God still keeps me and will keep you. For all who asked the question, "How do you do so much?" I say, "By following the leader, God!"

ঔ EIGHT ঔ

Wisdom from Grief

And I am convinced that nothing can ever separate us from God's love. Neither death nor life...

Romans 8:35 (NLT)

I have known grief many times. Each time it changed me in the immediate time after a death, but profoundly, over time. John Fawcett wrote in the *Daily Word*, May 28, 2007, "When we asunder part it gives us inward pain; but we shall still be joined in heart and hope to meet again." These words adequately reflect my experience over 14 years after my husband James died. The grieving of a loved one cannot be compared, in my view, with any other loss. Physical death is final, removing all opportunities for change. As we grieve, it is more likely than not that we will experience unfamiliar emotions, regrets, guilt - sometimes without cause - and feelings we can neither explain nor understand. If we are able to lean into these feelings, in time wisdom brings resolve.

Human touch after death is needed and it is wise to receive touch, being careful to receive it as your heart directs. Waiting is a wise choice, allowing a painful pause before making major changes. Waiting without knowing what is to come at times of death has inspired me to listen and wait as I reflect on Jesus' visit to Mary and Martha three days after their brother and a friend of Jesus died (John 11:33-36). Jesus' arrival time to support Mary and Martha paled to what He did. These sisters were bothered that Jesus had waited too long to come, yet His revelation to them forever changed them; Jesus brought Lazarus to life. But before He did:

> *One of the most touching scenes in the Bible is Jesus at the tomb of his dear friend Lazarus. Jesus raised Lazarus from the dead, but before doing so he did a very human and normal thing: he wept over the death of a friend.*
>
> (J. Stephen Lang)

I tried to define an appropriate mourning period after my husband died only to find that 14 years later, some days I am as sad as I was November 12, 2004. I still mourn! Immediately after James' funeral, I returned to serving/working, attending events, and dining out, among other activities -- each of which masked my pain but did nothing to begin my healing. I did find significant healing in crying, which some have said, "Is like an aspirin to a headache." Crying is uncomfortable for many; it tends to generate feelings of helplessness, even weakness. I cried often and for long periods, and gained comfort by Jesus' model. I try to remember not to tell people not to cry when saddened by loss. It is a gift to allow a person to cry without creating barriers of any kind. Crying stops when it has run its course. There is no time limit.

Mourning is not a time to show strength or to be expected to hide feelings. The work of grief is hard. The pain of loss is real even if the relationship had limitations. I remember an experience with an insurance adjuster that taught me much about death, relationships and responses. I called the insurance carrier who covered James' health insurance to notify them that he was dead. The adjuster offered condolences and then said, "Your loss is painful even though you may not have liked your husband." When I did not immediately respond he said, "Oh! I spoke inappropriately. I am so sorry." Even as he was out of line and wrong, his statement in some instances is truth. Grief however, must be engaged without impediments such as assumptions, opinions, overt helpful intentions, and platitudes.

About a month after James was buried, I was taking a walk in Washington Square Park when a neighbor caught up to me. He said, "I heard that your husband died. He was so sick and for a long time. He is better off now, gone to another home." This painful, ignorant comment was well-intentioned, and yet, insensitive to my feelings. This man did not know where James had gone and even if he did, I was not ready to hear his comment. I know James is in heaven but I did not want to hear that when I was grappling with the reality of his absence.

When offering condolences, try not to make assumptions, as did the insurance adjuster and my neighbor. These truths, as important as they may be, cannot be received while grieving. It is best to say as little as possible, avoiding the kind of message this insurance adjuster and neighbor unintentionally and incorrectly made. Condolences do not require us to make assumptions or commentary, only to respond to a loss. "I am sorry" or "I'm thinking of you" or best yet, if true, "I'm praying for you." It is insensitive to ask the cause of death. If a relationship is close, the person mourning the death is more likely to state the cause than not. Otherwise, it is not our business to know. For the person in pain, speaking the cause of death aloud may often help that person to move toward reality, but it is insensitive to ask.

Mourning is a process and only dissipates in its own time. I could work, but not as much and because my attention span was incredibly short, interests waned, and fatigue and irritability were constantly present. Trying to navigate my inner feeling as I responded to nurturing from family and friends caused spiritual conflict and guilt. I struggled to not appear ungrateful for help offered from others. Mourning does not leave emotional space for these challenges and recognizing that allowed me to find ways to receive from others that which I could handle without pushing them away. This lesson served to help me over the remainder of my years in how to receive gifts from others. I believe condolences and help from most people is intended to be a source of comfort. It should be understood that help should serve the grieving person and not ourselves.

My pain some days is as raw as it was on November 12, 2004, balanced by gratitude for having experienced James' never-ending love. I leaned into the loss of our relationship that was so deep, death has not separated its strength. Compassionate friends and social engagements have kept me from despair. Pushing people away is not wise. Those persons allowed to be close need to know you well enough not to be offended when your heart says, "leave me alone." Do not be afraid of the aloneness. These times free you to be angry, guilty, questioning, and to work through and into resolution, which can be tiring and does not need commentaries. Time alone is healing and allows for a closer connection with God. In silence, we hear the words of Jesus, "I will never leave you alone."

While I would have loved to have a healthy James alive, I would not have wanted him to stay in a body that had trapped his soul. As I looked to God after the first year of my husband's death, asking what was next, and what grief did for and in me, I received this message from Paul, writing to the church in Corinth:

> *All praise to the God and Father of our Master Jesus the Messiah! Father of all mercy! God of all healing counsel! He comes alongside us when we go through hard times, and before you know it, he brings us alongside someone else who*

> *is going through hard times so that we can be there for that person just as God was there for us [me].*
>
> 2 Corinthians1:3-4 (*The Message*).

Although our society is uncomfortable with death, wisdom informs that through weeping, mourning, enduring pain, the greatest strength to grieving is prayer. Wisdom gained in grief and waiting has allowed me to grow into a more focused servant to others who like me mourn the death of a loved one, especially a spouse. Grieving taught me all of us will ultimately cross that path. Grief led me to focus on and participate in the lives of others with love, as Fawcett writes, we will "meet again."

> *And then this: We can tell you with complete confidence—we have the Master's word on it—that when the Master comes again to get us, those of us who are still alive will not get a jump on the dead and leave them behind. In actual fact, they'll be ahead of us.*
>
> *The Master himself will give the command. Archangel thunder! God's trumpet blast!*
>
> *He'll come down from heaven and the dead in Christ will rise—they'll go first. Then the rest of us who are still alive at the time will be caught up with them into the clouds to meet the Master. Oh, we'll be walking on air! And then there will be one huge family reunion with the Master. So reassure one another with these words.*
>
> 1 Thessalonians 4:15-18 (*The Message*)

Thanks to Others

Writing this, my second book speaking to wisdom gained through the lens of my 86 years of life has been a reflective process. My spiritual growth has been more significant than I can articulate. As wisdom and discernment has increased, I am even more aware of the gifts from friends with whom I share my journey. I am tremendously grateful to Mary T. Garrett whose walk beside me has been encouraging, prodding, remembering, attentive to details, editing and correcting, typing and changing, and most importantly, loving. Without Mary, there would not be A Privileged Life II - Wisdom from my Journey. My Christian daughter, Mary, more than most, knows my inner core from a journey we have traveled over 45 years. I am so very grateful to and for Mary. She is a busy person, yet across months of this work, she has made it feel effortless. Thank you, Mary. A gem to my journey.

I am grateful to the friends who willingly read the manuscript, offered edits, advice and encouragement. Four years ago, I began a journey with Presidents and Deans of Historic Black Seminaries, spending considerable time with theologians, men whose daily lives are devoted to preparing women and men to build the kingdom of God. Three of my friends, Dr. Alton B. Pollard, Dr. Vergel Lattimore and Dr. Edward Wheeler, read my manuscript, validating the authenticity of that journey. I am truly grateful to them. As grateful as I am for their contributions, I am abundantly blessed by their sharing of personal relationships in Christ, which continues to enrich my life.

I prayed for direction as I captured my thoughts and scripted memories, asking many times, "Who should read?" In the quiet of my spirit came names of the men above, along with Amy Kardash, Eve Higginbotham, Lynette Brown-Sow, Dixie James, Letty Piper, Rosie Hsueh, Mike Pulsifer, and Emerson and Abby Brisbon. I don't know the reason I was spiritually directed to these special ones, but as one who has grown in obedience to the inner Spirit, I requested their help and they generously responded. I am most grateful to each of them for taking the reading task, validating their experiences with me and their reflections as they read. I acknowledge these relationships with gratitude.

When I wrote my first book, my friend, spiritual sister, and Sociology Professor helped to articulate the language which clarified, expanded and added to my work. Dr. Renée C. Fox and I have traveled together a very long time. My late husband, James always wanted us to "write something" together. And so, Renée's reflections on A Privileged Life II - Wisdom From My Journey meets his request and honors me. Thank you, Renee, for our friendship shared over an extended period, with admiration and affection.

Finally, I am grateful for my children, those genetic, Edgar and Nancy, and Bret, who is my gift of a son. They, with many others, have encouraged and expressed love at every junction.

Thank you!!

A Perspective

In her words, Delores Brisbon invited me to "place a note" in her book -- an invitation that I consider to be an honor.

When I first came to know her in 1969, Delores was already the Supervisor of Nursing at the University of Pennsylvania, and I was a newly recruited professor in the University's departments of sociology, psychiatry and medicine. She is a nurse. I am a sociologist. She is Black. I am White. She is Christian. I am Jewish. Ostensibly, what we initially had in common was the fact that I am chiefly a sociologist of medicine, and that I had the privilege of being one of her daughter's teachers when she was a Penn undergraduate. But Delores and her husband James welcomed me into their family. And over time, I came to feel that she is a sister, with whom I am linked spiritually, as well as intellectually and professionally.

However, I am not Delores' spiritual equal. At the age of 91—a few years older than she is—I have not achieved in the course of my life journey the spiritual wisdom, insight, conviction and courage that she has. But her example helps to light my path as I wrestle with the challenges that being elderly entails. And in writing this, I not only pay tribute to her spiritual stature, but I am thankful for the significance of her example. And I also feel that I am fulfilling a message that I implicitly received from her beloved husband James, that someday she and I might "say something together."

Renée C. Fox, Ph.D.
Professor Emeritus
Department of Sociology
University of PA
Philadelphia, PA

Acknowledgments of the Work of Others and Copyrights

Every effort has been made to ensure that the words of others are recognized and credited in the narrative of this book. If anyone has been missed, it is not intentional. If so, please tell me: PrivilegedLife@comcast.net.

Scriptures and quotes are listed in order of appearance in each narrative chapter. Translations are indicated in parentheses.

- Quotes credited to Mark Nepo from The Book of Awakening, Copyright 2000. First published by Conari Press, an imprint of Red Wheeler/Weiser LLC. Used by permission.

- Quotes credited to Oswald Chambers are from My Utmost for His Highest, the updated edition in today's language, edited by James Riemann, Copyright 1992 by Oswald Chambers Publications Association, Ltd. Original Edition Copyright 1935 by Dodd, Mead & Company. Copyright renewed 1963 by Oswald Chambers Publications Association Ltd. Used by permission.

- Quotes by Robertson, Pusey, Barr & Martineau are from Mary W. Tileston's 1977 printing, Daily Strength for Daily Needs

- Quotes credited to J. Stephen Lang are from The Complete Book of Bible Promises, Copyright 1997. Used by permission of Tyndale House Publishers, Inc., Wheaton, IL.

Introduction

Mark Nepo - The Book of Awakening - Having the Life You Want by Being Present to the Life You Have (Quotations) Copyright 2000
Luke 1:3 (TNIV)
John 17- cited; no verses
Proverbs 22:2
Deuteronomy 5:16

Chapter 1 - The Bible – Our Only Source of Wisdom

Mark Nepo - The Book of Awakening (Quotations)
Oswald Chambers - My Utmost for His Highest (Quotations)
J. Stephen Lang - All the Promises of The Bible (Scriptures by categories) Proverbs 11:8 (NLT)
Dr. Chris Hall, President, Regent Seminary (Quote)
Matthew 22:37 (The Message)

C.S. Lewis (Quote)
2 Timothy 3:16 (Amplified Bible)
Genesis 1; 2:13; 6, 7, 8:6-22 (NIV)
Deuteronomy 5
Genesis 22:1-19 (NIV)
Jean Nicolas Grou (Quote)
Proverbs 3:5-6 (Amplified Bible)
Jeremiah 29:11 (NIV)
1 Corinthians 4:20 (NLT)
Matthew 17:20 (NLT)
Hebrews 11:1-2 (The Message)
1 Kings 3:7-12 (NIV)
1 Corinthians 1:19-21, 25-27; 3:19-20 (INIV)
Isaiah 42:16 (RSV)
Luke 15:10 (NLT) Isaiah 43:19 (INIV)
Philippians 2:3 (RSV)

Chapter 2 - Wisdom From Prayer

Philippians 4: 6b, 7a (NLT)
Psalm 139:4 (NIV)
Proverb 1:7 (Message)
Hebrew 4:16 (NLT)
Eugene Peterson, Praying with the Psalms (Quote)
Oswald Chambers (Quote)
Romans 8:26 (NIV)
Isaiah 65:24 (NIV)
J. Pennington (Quote)
Mark 1:35 (NIV)

Matthew 6:5-7(NIV)
Edgar J. Hoover (Quote)

Chapter 3 - Wisdom of Being Yourself

Matthew 5:5 (The Message) Mark Nepo (Quote)
Ecclesiastes 6:9 (NIV)
1 Corinthians 12; Romans 12 (Cited, no verses)
The Doctrine of the Mean (Quote)

Chapter 4 - Wisdom From Marriage

J. Stephen Lang, All of the Promises in the Bible (Quote)
Time Alone With God, Devotional Reading December 22nd
Ephesians 5:31 (NIV)
Mark Twain (Quote)
Psalm 127:3a
Ephesians 6:4b (NIV)
1 Corinthians 13:4-8 (The Message)
J. Stephen Lang (Quote)

Chapter 5 - Wisdom From Racism

Lillie E. Barr (Quote)
Proverbs 3:5-6 (NIV)
Psalms 139:14a (NIV)
F.W. Roberson (Quote) 1816-1859

James Martineau (Quote) 1805-1900 Eugene Peterson (Quote)
Jeremiah 29:11(NIV)
Oswald Chambers (Quote)
E.B. Pusey (Quote) 1800-1882

Chapter 6 – Wisdom of Leadership

Proverbs 13:4a

Chapter 7 - Wisdom of Aging

Proverbs 6:31 (NIV)
Psalms 90:10 (NIV)
Genesis 5:22; 6:9-22 (Cited)
Deuteronomy 34:7 (NIV)
Psalms 92:14 (NIV)
Proverbs 20:29

Chapter 8 - Wisdom From Grief

Romans 8:35 (NLT)
John Fawcett, Daily Bread Devotional Quote
J. Stephen Lang, All the Promises of the Bible (Quote)
2 Corinthians 1:3-4 (The Message)
1 Thessalonians 4:15-18 (The Message)

About the Author

Delores Flynn Brisbon is a widow, mother of two adult genetic children and four adults whose relationship is akin to mother. She is grandmother to six; three genetic and three gifted to her thorough relationships. Delores is a community leader and advocate for children, black boys in particular. She is an Elder in the First Presbyterian Church in Philadelphia.

For over a sixty-year period, Delores has served more than fifty organizations whose missions are service to health, higher education, or non-profits focused on human kind as Trustee or Director. Currently she is President of the Board of Directors of the Presbyterian Community Ministries of Delaware Valley (PCMDV), a ministry designed to build resilience in black boys through loving human connections.

Her professional career spans more than sixty years. Now retired from professional health care, Delores served as a nurse supervisor at the John Andrew Memorial Hospital, Tuskegee, Alabama; Director of Nurses, Flint Goodridge Hospital, New Orleans, Louisiana; Head

Nurse, Supervisor, Strategist, and Chief Operating Officer (COO) at the Hospital of the University of Pennsylvania, Philadelphia, Pennsylvania. Delores was the first black woman appointed to the position of COO during the Civil Rights struggle of the 1950-60s. She has served as Consultant to specific initiatives for the City of Philadelphia, the Hospital and Higher Education Authority, and as a Master to the Court on a matter of church negotiations. Currently, Delores serves the In Trust Center for Theological Education as a Senior Advisor.

This book is a sequel to Delores' first book, A Privileged Life – Remembering My Journey, which was a memoir written almost ten years ago.

Delores lives in Philadelphia, Pennsylvania.

Delores F. Brisbon